MUSH!

A BEGINNER'S MANUAL
OF SLED DOG TRAINING

Edited by Bella Levorsen
for the SIERRA NEVADA DOG DRIVERS, INCORPORATED

D1557223

Third Edition - 1997

Sales and Distribution...

Barkleigh Productions, Inc.
6 State Rd. #113
Mechanicsburg PA 17055
(717) 691-3388 • Fax (717) 691-3381
E-mail: barkleigh@aol.com

DEDICATION

TUFFY

To Tuffy, renowned leader from Huslia, Alaska. Unique in ability, aloof in personality. It was my privilege to know him.

Bella Levorsen

(Original photographer unknown. Photo copy from Alaska Dog Racing News by Mark Levorsen)

CONTENTS

ILLUSTRATIONS

PREFACE

Teams of working sled dogs started hauling supplies and performing rescue missions in the Sierra Nevada mountains in the late 1800s. These teams started racing for pleasure and purse in the 1920s, with "Scotty" Allan's son George driving a team and Jack London a frequent spectator. Many silent movies about dog teams were made in Truckee during this time. Races have been held in the northern California area almost every year ever since.

In 1961, 10 racers got together to form the Sierra Nevada Dog Drivers. More and more people joined the group until now the membership stands at about 100. The club has always cooperated with other sled dog organizations, being a member of the early Western Dog Mushers Association and sending a representative, Roger Reitano, to the organizational meeting of the International Sled Dog Racing Association at Niagara Falls in 1966. Since the beginning, the Sierra Nevada Dog Drivers has been a member and strong supporter of the International Sled Dog Racing Association, even providing it with its president. Robert Levorsen, its President from 1971 to 1974 and its Chairman of the Board from 1989 to 1992.

In 1970, Mrs. Mel Fishback, Mrs. Pat Daniels and Mrs. Betty Allen thought it a good idea to write a few mimeographed sheets of instructions to help the ever increasing number of beginners in the local club get started running their dogs. Questions commonly asked would be answered in writing instead of verbally. That was how the first edition of *Mush!* came into being. Since then the written instructions, like the club and the sport in general, have grown in size and scope.

This third edition of Mush has made use of the varied

knowledge of many people both within the club and all over the country. Contributions of people outside the club are acknowledged in the main text of the book. Within the club, in addition to the editors, members who have contributed are:

Thom Ainsworth	Georgene Goodstein	Randy Roe
Lucy Bettis	Nancy Link	Roxie Varvaro
Pat Daniels	Tom & Sylvia Palmer	Dave Walling
Dave Decker	George Ricard	Daphne Rippon

Various quotes and references which have been taken from published works are given credit adjacent to the excerpts throughout the book. In addition, much information has been taken from *Team and Trail* with the kind permission of Cindy Molburg and "Uncle Elmer". Special recognition must go to George Attla for all the knowledge he has given the editors through his book and his personal communications.

Photographs have come from a variety of sources, all of which the editors acknowledge with thanks. Outstanding in this department is Mally Hilands, who — for love of photography and dog mushers — has for years stood on snowy sled dog trails taking pictures of all who came along.

While the drawings in the first edition of *Mush!* were done by Mel Fishback, many of them were re-drawn for this edition by Georgene Goodstein, who also did all of the new illustrations.

A special thanks must go to Marion Rippon, detective story author for Doubleday & Company and professor of creative writing at the University of Victoria, British Columbia. Though not involved with the sport in any way, she checked most of the finished manuscript for content, organization and grammar. In short, she taught the editors how to write more professionally than they had done previously.

To all those who helped, the Sierra Nevada Dog Drivers say, "Thank you!"

Bella Levorsen, Editor
Robert Levorsen, Associate Editor

Robyn Murer, Associate Editor
Committee Members:
Joel Fruchtman

Novato, California, October 1975

Harmon Peeke

HOW TO USE
THIS BOOK

This book is primarily about how to train a dog to become a member of a racing team. It is aimed first of all at the beginner who has had no experience whatsoever. But it is also aimed at the person who has been running dogs a few years in the hope that he can learn some aspects of the sport that he did not know before. A few chapters that have nothing to do with racing have been added with the thought that some people may want to use their dogs for some other or additional form of recreation.

Since this book undertakes to answer the questions most commonly asked by beginners, the material has been arranged so that the answers to those questions will be easy to find. For that reason it is organized in areas: sled dog lore; dogs; equipment; training; riding the sled; a variety of miscellaneous, unrelated subjects; and ends with a section on health and nutrition. The Appendix contains the Sierra Nevada Dog Driver's Instructions for Checkers.

Areas are divided into as many separate chapters as are warranted. Since the book is intended to be a reference work, all chapters stand on their own and are self contained. To further help the reader refer back to a specific point, some chapters are subdivided, and all subjects have headings and sub-headings.

It is hoped that you, the reader, will enjoy this book and find it useful. The Sierra Nevada Dog Drivers welcome you to the sport.

SLED DOG LORE

Sled dog racing began as a formal sport with the first All-Alaska Sweepstakes race in 1908. The Nome Kennel Club was formed to organize and sponsor the race. Rules and principles of racing established by this club are still being used today, with little modification, in most races throughout the world.

The All-Alaska Sweepstakes races were run in early April from Front Street in Nome, across the Seward Peninsula to Candle and back, a round trip distance of 408 miles. It was a true test of men and teams as the trail went from "sea ice to high mountains, with rivers, tundra, timber, glaciers, and everything else in the way of mental and physical hardships en route. . .even Old Death Valley that was nearly always filled with a smoking blizzard, no matter how fine the weather was on both sides." (A. A. "Scotty" Allan, *Gold, Men and Dogs,* G. P. Putnam's Sons, New York, Copyright 1931, p. 178.)

The dogs involved in the first Sweepstakes were regular freighting teams, and the harnesses and sleds were freighting types. For the second running of the race, "Scotty" Allan designed a 30 pound racing sled with long runners and a curved handle bar, instead of upright posts, to allow pedaling. Each dog's harness and towline weighed only 14 ounces. (George Allan, "Scotty's" son, personal communication.)

Dog types changed too. Huskies were imported from Siberia; and with "Iron Man" Johnson as driver, they set a record in 1910 of 74 hours, 14 minutes and 37 seconds. This record stood throughout the series.

In 1911 "Scotty" Allan won the race with Alaskan crossbreeds (mostly Malamute—Setter crosses) in just over 80

A. A. ("Scotty") Allan
Frontispiece of *Gold, Men and Dogs*, with special permission from
G. P. Putnam's Sons. (Photo copy by Mark Levorsen)

hours through blizzard conditions. Allan raced in eight Sweepstakes; won three, was second in three, and was third twice.

Another early sled dog racing "great" was the Norwegian immigrant Leonhard Seppala. He, too, got his start driving a freight team; but for racing, he used only the smaller Siberian huskies. When the First World War forced cancellation of further Sweepstakes, he had also won three victories. Seppala went on later to win many shorter races in Alaska and in New England. His Siberians became the forerunner of the American Kennel Club registered Siberian husky breed.

While in New England, Seppala gave one of his dogs to a young veterinary student named Roland Lombard. Not only did "Doc" Lombard earn his way through college by racing a small sled dog team (4 — 5 dogs), but he continued racing,

Leonhard Seppala and Togo

Togo, ". . .the most famous lead dog in Alaska at that time" (Ungermann, Kenneth A., *The Race to Nome,* p. 56) was elected to the Knik, Alaska Musher's Hall of Fame along with Leonhard Seppala. (Original photograph belonged to Rowland Bowles, Photo copy from Team and Trail, with permission, by Mark Levorsen)

training and improving methods until his death in 1990. He won eight Anchorage World Championships and contributed greatly to the sport. He was the first president of the International Sled Dog Racing Association, holding that position for five years.

Another "great" in current sled dog training and racing is George Attla, an Athabascan Indian from Huslia, and now Fairbanks, Alaska. George has won 10 Anchorage World Championships (more than any other musher) plus many other major races across the country. His book, Everything I Know About Training and Racing Sled Dogs, Arner Publications, Rome, N.Y., is out of print but is still considered the "Bible" for professional sled dog drivers throughout the world..

Dr. Roland Lombard with Ring and Nellie
Nellie, the dog with brown eyes under Doc's left arm, was elected to
the Knik, Alaska Mushers Hall of Fame along with Dr. Lombard.
(Photo courtesy of Mrs. Roland Lombard)

Both George Attla and Dr. Roland Lombard, along with Leonhard Seppala and "Scotty" Allan, are among the handful of mushers honored in the Knik, Alaska Mushers' Hall of Fame. Seppala's leader Togo, plus Attla and Lombard's leader Nellie, were the first dogs so honored.

Races today are often put on by civic groups as well as by dog racing clubs. Since races take much time, hard work and money to organize, they have a way of coming and going as the enthusiasm of the sponsoring group waxes and wanes over the years. Some races, however, such as the Anchorage World Championship and the Fairbanks North American, have been in existence so many years, it seems likely they will go on forever.

George Attla
On the Yukon River, July, 1974. (Photo courtesy of George Attla)

Today's race events can have several different classes racing on the same weekend. Limited class races have trail lengths which depend on the maximum number of dogs in the teams. The unlimited class has no limit to the numbers of dogs in the teams, which usually varies from 12-20. Unlimited class trails are naturally much longer with trail lengths varying from 10 to 30 miles each day. Races are most often run in two heats on two consecutive days of a single weekend. Some of the biggest races will add a third heat on Friday. The combined time of all heats wins.

Long distance races of 100 miles and more, requiring camping out, are becoming increasingly popular. The Iditarod race in Alaska from Anchorage to Nome is the first of the modern long distance races. The trail is over 1,000 miles and takes at least 10 days to run, even in the best of weather.

Almost all states, provinces and European countries in the snow belt have sled dogs being exercised in harness, and most hold regular races Anyone wishing to have his dog pull a sled should have no trouble finding a congenial group already involved in the sport. These groups relive the thrills of their predecessors: the early Sweepstakes racers; the gold rush freighters, or "dog-punchers," of the 19th century; before them, the French voyageurs on their fur-gathering trips throughout Canada; and all of the Eskimos and Indians of the North who have been using sled dogs since beyond the reaches of recorded history.

George at home, 1992
(Photo by Bob Levorsen

KINDS OF
SLED DOGS

A common misconception about sled dogs is that they must be northern breed dogs of great size. Many newcomers to racing, expecting to see only beautiful teams of 100 pound huskies, are surprised at the variety of breeds represented at a race, and even more surprised at the small size of the average sled dog.

Almost any dog can be taught to pull, and any medium-sized one can make a satisfactory sled dog. Many mushers new to the sport will use the breed which they already own as a matter of preference and convenience. Thus, German shepherds, Dalmatians, Dobermans and collies can be seen in harness. Several winning teams consist solely of non-northern breeds such as Irish setters, and the list of cross-bred dogs used to pull sleds today would be endless.

Strength is not as important in sled dog racing as speed since the sled load is distributed among many dogs. Large, heavily built dogs with great strength are not as fast as lean, wiry dogs; and they tend to tire sooner when asked to go fast. Human weight lifters don't run in marathon races.

The most important requirement for a good sled dog is the desire to run. Fortunately, most dogs enjoy running. Other requirements are good build, good health and good training.

NORTHERN BREEDS
Northern breed dogs have been used for thousands of years by Arctic people as work dogs, hunters, reindeer herders, companions, guardians and sled pullers. Through time, separate ethnic groups have developed their own strains

of dogs, most of which have been given the English name of the people with whom they were found. The white Samoyed dogs so popular with early European Arctic and Antarctic explorers were developed by the Samoyed peoples of east central Siberia as reindeer herders; the Alaskan Malamute was developed by the Malemuit (Mahlemut) Eskimos of northwestern Alaska for hauling heavy loads long distances. Even the husky breeds were named after the people that developed them, for the early North American explorers called the Eskimos they encountered the "huskies" because of their solid build. Thus, we have the Greenland husky, the Mackenzie River husky, the Alaskan husky, and the Siberian husky.

The Siberian husky was imported in the early 1900s for racing in the All-Alaska Sweepstakes and did so well there and later in New England that this breed is the most common purebred, registered dog on the sled dog race trails. The Alaskan husky, like the Indian or village dog of central Alaska, has a varied breed background, though the husky type dog predominates, with a little wolf mixed in for stamina. These dogs have been specifically bred for working, hauling game and belongings on sleds, and for running traplines in the interior. They make excellent race dogs and can stand either cold or warm weather. Most winning teams have at least some of these native Alaskan dogs on them.

OTHER BREEDS

For pure speed, the coursing hounds, fastest dogs on earth, would seem to be most desirable. But speed without the stamina to maintain it mile after mile does not count for much, so the greyhounds, the Salukis, the Afghans and the borzois are not found in purebred form on the race trails. On the other hand, the moderately fast, long distance hounds developed for tracking coons for days on end have won many races, particularly in moderate to warm weather conditions. Many crosses of husky and greyhound have been attempted, often with great success, particularly in eastern Canada.

Bird dogs have also been tried as sled dogs, with the Irish setter doing outstandingly well. These long-haired, long-legged dogs are fast and strong and were used to haul mail in the American Northwest in the 1920s and 30s and to win races in the 30s and 40s. They are still running and winning races today, sometimes as full teams, sometimes with an Irish setter leading a team of Alaskan huskies.

Setter crosses have been popular for years, particularly in Alaska. An Idaho cross with a stag hound has been named the Targhee hound after nearby mountains. Fairbanks mushers have been notably successful in crossing the Irish setter with Alaskan huskies and reportedly even with wolves and Targhees.

JOHN HENDERSON AND IRISH SETTERS
Shown here racing at Sisters, Oregon, 1975 with two-year-old Toto in lead and 12-year-olds Buzzard and Zip in wheel. This team won the 1975 International Sled Dog Racing Association's Silver Medal for the Five Dog Class. (Photo by "Mally" Hilands)

ACQUIRING
A RACING DOG

An integral part of dog racing is the acquiring of dogs. This occurs at every level of the sport, whether it be a novice driver upgrading his present team, perhaps moving to a larger class, or the professional driver wishing to maintain his achieved level of winning performance. Buying a dog can have its pitfalls, especially for the less experienced driver who hasn't learned his way around the "dog scene" yet. To quote Swenson:

"When I first went to Siberia and began buying dogs, I decided that I wanted a sporty-looking outfit. I made up my mind that I would have a white team, composed of especially large, fine, well-matched animals, with fine red harnesses and red sleds. I was going to be cock of the trail and show those natives how fine an outfit could look. I could see that the natives were amused, but they hunted up the dogs all right, and I got my white team. It looked like a million dollars. . .but as a sled team it was no good at all. There were a few good dogs in it, but before long I replaced half of the team with dogs which had stamina and speed and intelligence. For years the natives kidded me about the white team. They'd laugh and say, 'Swenson wants a white dog. He doesn't care whether it's good or bad; he just wants a white dog.'"
(Olaf Swenson, *Northwest of the World,* Dodd, Mead and Co., New York, 1944, page 188)

Possibly the best way to buy the right dog the first time is to get advice from experienced drivers with good dogs. These drivers should become acquainted with you and your driving abilities in order to be in a fair position to offer their help in the purchase of dogs, whether from them directly or through their referrals to other kennels. Local sled dog club newsletters and international mushing publications often have advertisements of sled dogs for sale. They also contain race results that give the prospective buyer a chance to learn how the drivers with dogs for sale have placed in competition.

When buying a dog, there are a few general rules of thumb to keep in mind. Don't expect perfection; it's not for sale. Know the seller as much as possible, and make sure the seller knows the buyer's needs. Big-name kennel dogs are fine, but don't forget the smaller kennel with the same stock.

Dogs can be purchased by personal visit to a kennel; but more often, because of the expensive distances involved, new animals are acquired through letter or telephone transactions. The novice buyer need not hesitate to purchase the dog sight unseen in this manner. You are purchasing performance, not looks. So unless you want a dog that has a particular kind of appearance, there is no need to see it beforehand. You can neither tell much about a dog's performance by examining him in a kennel nor learn much by driving him yourself only once. You have to take the owner's word for his ability. What you can check on is the owner's reputation as a driver and as a person. Most drivers will be completely honest with you because they want you to be satisfied with the dog. Their reputation is at stake.

It is critical during buying inquiries that the prospective buyer be completely honest as to his present team's level of performance and potential, especially regarding speed, and be realistic as to what he expects to gain through the purchase.

In order to fit the dog to the buyer, the seller should have certain information. As the buyer, you should be completely honest with the seller when informing him about the following:

Your Present Kennel
    Breed of dogs
    Sex of dogs, particularly your leader

Size of your team now
How dogs are housed

Your Expectations
From new dog
Position you want new dog to run
Planned team size

Your Experience
Your patience limitations
What class you have raced in
Where you placed

Your Training Methods
Type of trail
If you use a cart
Number of miles in your usual training run

If you are looking for a lead dog, remember that there are two kinds: a) the trail leader who stays in front and strings the team out, and b) the command leader who both stays out front and takes commands.

When you see an advertisement or hear of a leader for sale, be sure to find out which kind it is. Also find out what size team this dog has led, if it has actually raced, in what races, and where the team placed. A leader who has placed 10th in front of 16 dogs in a major race will be a better leader than one who once led two other dogs around the block.

Sometimes an older and reliable command leader who is no longer fast enough to stay in front of a big team is just what a small, beginning team needs to keep it out of trouble and to give its new dogs experience. These older leaders are less expensive than dogs in their prime, particularly if the owner is interested in placing them in a good home.

If you are looking for a registered purebred of *any* of the northern breeds, keep in mind that being a purebred will not automatically make it a first-class sled dog. As with all dogs,

what counts is the proven performance of that particular dog
and the racing record of its entire line.
When you are buying a puppy, you will not, of course, have
any running record to go by. You can only go by the puppy's
line. You pay your money and you take your chances.
The buyer is entitled to and should obtain certain information from the seller about any dog. The information should
include:

Vital Statistics
   Sex
   Age
   Breeding lines; registration, if any
   Physical appearance; size
   Speed
   Temperament
   Any behavior peculiarities (i.e. destroys doghouse)

Medical and Nutritional
   Past serious illness
   Any chronic illness
   Any medications being administered at present time (i.e.
   caracide for heartworm
   Status of rabies and distemper shots
   Last worming; for what type worms
   Any feeding problems
   Type and amount of food being used

Training
   Stage of training
   Trained by a man or a woman
   Discipline used and required
   Size of team usually run with
   Position dog runs best
   Side preferred
   Whether runs better alone or with companion
   Type of trail usually run

Any experience in front of a cart
Number of miles in recent training runs
Approximate miles put on this season

Racing Experience
What races
What class
Position team usually places (approximate)
Kennel's first or second string
Years of racing

The talking done, a purchase made, the buyer, especially the novice, now waits in anticipation for the new arrival. It is well to remember that one's first dog bought for performance does not always bring Mr. Sociability or Show Dog of the Century to your doorstep. Performance is what was purchased. Regarding performance, it is important to *let the animal get used to its new surroundings and new driver before putting it into the team.* It is a rare dog that will go from crate to harness, particularly in lead position, and give a peak performance. To illustrate, another quote from *Northwest of the World:*

"I shall never forget Billkoff (Snowball in English), the finest dog I have ever known. . .I met him many years ago when he belonged to a native, and I wanted him ten minutes after I had seen him. It was not only for his record as a leader, but his personality, his character and his wisdom. . .and I found myself wanting him more than I had ever wanted any other dog. I tried to buy him, but his native owner had as much appreciation of a good dog as I had and would not sell him. Completely courteous, however, he would never come out frankly and tell me that he thought too much of the dog himself to let me have him, but always gave me another reason, saying, 'I don't think that dog would be any good for you. He is too used to me. He wouldn't mind anyone else.' "

Several years later, Swenson got Billkoff and continues:

"When I started out to work with the dog, I discovered that the native's spoken reason for not selling him had been more than a stall. For six months, he was the worst dog I had ever known. He simply refused to accept me as his boss and constantly took matters in his own hands. Finally, however, he gave up the struggle and from then until the day he died (several years later) he was the best dog I had ever seen in any man's team." (Swenson, op. cit. page 183.)

There are a hundred reasons for initial disappointment in the performance of a newly acquired dog. To name a few:

The dog has never run with a cart and is afraid of it.

Running conditions vary from area to area, and the dog may never have experienced super-fast hard trails or deep snow conditions.

The dog is just plain scared and needs time to get over it.

The dog doesn't understand the new driver's commands; is frightened by his motions, voice, correction or training methods.

The dog is in poor condition from the sudden change in food, altitude, climate, water, etc.

The dog is not used to a male (or female) driver.

And so on.

Resist the temptation to receive a new dog and put him immediately in any position of stress. Even if he is an experienced leader, being in lead is always a position of stress. And with new dogs behind him, he doesn't know if they are following him or chasing him! Too often good leaders have been completely ruined by being put in lead immediately upon arrival. A high-priced dog does not react like a high-priced automobile. So for the first few runs, put the leader behind your old one. After those runs, put him in double lead, preferably with a dog of the opposite sex. Wait a long time before you put him in single lead.

It is difficult to tell whether a buyer has made a good or bad deal. Here are some general guidelines that might be kept in mind: If soon after arrival a dog is proven to have some physical illness or disability that your veterinarian says *must* have been present *before* the purchase, the buyer has just reason to inform the seller about it. If the dog, after a reasonable time to become adjusted, shows intolerable aggression in harness towards other dogs, the buyer likewise has reason to complain. Also, if after a reasonable time to become adjusted, the dog when in harness does nothing but lie on his stomach and will not get up and run in any fashion, the buyer should complain to the seller.

There are other, lesser reasons for the buyer to be unhappy with a newly purchased dog. The dog may not keep his line tight. He may duck into the bush or under the truck at every opportunity. He may even not want to come out of his dog box. A leader may not take commands. If he is a known good dog, then it is reasonable to assume that the dog needs more time for adjustment. Remember that many times, even a GOOD dog needs up to a full season with a new driver to turn in a superb performance. Judgement cannot be passed on him until the SECOND season.

Or the driver, particularly if he is a new driver in his own second or third season, may be doing something wrong. If the dog initially gives good runs and then deteriorates, it indicates that the driver is at fault and needs help.

To get help, the driver should not hesitate to contact the seller to discuss the matter. The former owner, in most instances, should be in a fairly good position to offer helpful hints. The new owner should also ask the advice of experienced drivers close at hand who have observed both him and the dog in action. Perhaps they can see something that he does not.

It should always be remembered, however, that unless it was agreed between buyer and seller beforehand that the dog was sent on trial, there are no refunds or exchanges in the dog business. A dog is not merchandise with a "completely satis-

fied or your money back" guarantee. Your best guarantee is
to be honest with yourself and the seller and to not expect a
miracle. Then if you don't like the dog after a season's trial,
just don't deal with that seller again.

Enlarging a race kennel through breeding does not really
fit under the heading "Acquiring a Racing Dog," but perhaps
a discussion of breeding versus buying would be helpful here.

Money considerations may not be realized, as money is
doled out in dribbles rather than in one lump sum. When outside breeding is sought, it can involve a stud fee. Once the
puppies are whelped, they must be fed for some time before
they are of age to race. Taking a minimum of 30 cents worth
of food per day per puppy comes to approximately $100 a
year a pup, with no guarantee it will make the team. This does
not include food supplements, shots, or other medical care
which might be needed. Breeding also unfortunately involves
selection of the animals to be bred. Genetics contain a fair
amount of unknowns as well as innumerable possibilities.
With higher caliber teams, this can greatly reduce the usable
pups from a litter. A breeder, at best, may get only two to
three out of six puppies which can make his team.

The above statements are made by way of comparison and
are not meant to discourage breeding, but only to point out
that while breeding with care and planning is both desirable
and necessary, it is not necessarily the cheapest, fastest, or
most reliable way to build a team.

Keep all of this in mind when you gasp at the price of a
trained sled dog. You may be lucky and find someone who,
for personal reasons, must sell first-class dogs for less, but ordinarily pups of good breeding will run between $100 to $200.
Good team dogs start at about $250 and go up. Leaders will
start about $500 and go up to almost anywhere. The very best
leaders, if you ever find one for sale, usually come in package
deals where the buyer must buy several dogs to get the leader.
These deals can run into the thousands. You are buying years
of experience, training, selective breeding, and in a way, all
the dogs who didn't make it. Considering all of this, the price
doesn't seem so high.

If you do not have the money and are a gambler, one way to get additional dogs cheap is from your local pound. Many first-class racing dogs have been discovered in the pound. Discuss with your humane society director what you are looking for, and it may not be long before he will have a dog or two for you.

Wherever you acquire your dog, be sure to give it kindness, understanding, good care and time.

CONFINEMENT and HOUSING OF SLED DOGS

Many ways of confining sled dogs are possible. The type you will use will depend upon the number of dogs, the space available, and the amount of money you want to spend.

Every dog should have a house or a bed that is his own to give him a feeling of security and permanence. His house should give protection from rain or snow storms in the winter and from rain and hot sun in the summer.

CONFINING WITH CHAINS

Most large kennel owners secure their dogs with chains. This is the cheapest method and takes up the least space. Each dog needs five or six feet of chain with a swivel snap at one end to attach to the collar. The other end is fastened permanently, preferably with another swivel attachment, to a variety of objects.

PRECAUTIONS

With all systems, it is important to keep the dogs far enough apart so that they cannot reach each other. Although the owner, out of the kindness of his heart, thinks it would be nice for neighboring dogs to be able to play with each other, he should never risk the chance of fights, accidental breedings, or the dogs' being hurt or strangled by tangled chains.

CONFINING WITH RUNS

Small kennel owners often prefer runs, if they can afford them, because they don't like to keep their dogs chained. Large kennel owners may have a few runs for special dogs in

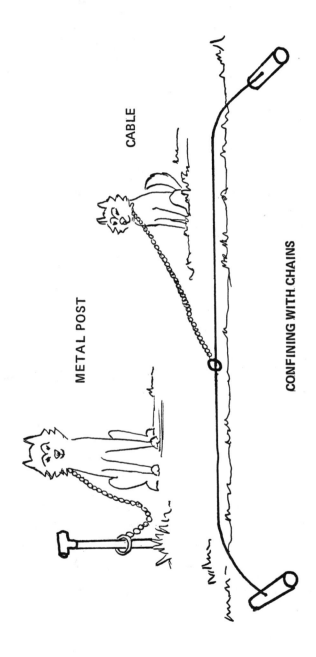

addition to the chains. Most all owners have fenced enclosures for puppies.

Runs vary in size, but all are long and narrow instead of square so that the dogs can get more exercise.

DOG HOUSES

If a dog is housed outside, he must have some kind of weatherproof shelter — usually a separate wooden house for each dog. Sometimes in the middle of Alaska a long, low communal lean-to is used. The dogs are chained to the posts that hold it up. On the northern coast of Alaska, where wood is scarce, discarded metal oil drums are used.

3' x 2' SIDE	4' x 2' ROOF	1' x 2' FRONT
3' x 2' SIDE	3' x 2' FLOOR	2' x 2' BACK

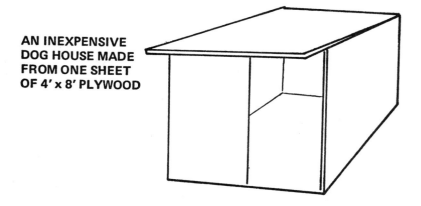

AN INEXPENSIVE DOG HOUSE MADE FROM ONE SHEET OF 4' x 8' PLYWOOD

SHARING YOUR OWN HOUSE

Legitimate questions usually asked about dogs living loose in the house are, "Won't the dogs get spoiled and not want to run? Isn't it necessary to keep them chained so that they will want to run when they are allowed to in harness?" Experience has shown that the answer to both questions is "No".

The dogs get more exercise walking around a house and yard than they do when they are chained. This exercise is good for them and seems to enhance their desire to run. In the summer when the dogs are not in training, this exercise helps keep them in shape.

Other advantages are that you and your dogs will develop better communication when you are living together, and they will develop better communication with each other. Then again, the dogs will become more socialized if they come in contact with all the people who come into the house. This helps them to be less nervous when they are exposed to strange people at the race site and on the trail.

Another plus is that if the dogs ever get completely loose, they are less motivated to take off and be gone for a week.

But best of all, when you are living in close contact with your dogs, you can tell immediately when one of them is not feeling well, and you can watch him more carefully than if he were chained to a dog house. An illness spotted quickly is much easier to cure, and prompt treatment saves the dog a lot of misery, maybe even his life, as in cases of bloat.

On the negative side, other than the continual cleaning up of dog hairs, is the possibility of a fight. You must have the facility to separate certain dogs when feeding, when a bitch is in season, and when you are gone from the house.

COLLARS

BUCKLE COLLARS

The simplest collar for sled dog use is one with an adjustable buckle, similar to a man's belt. It should have a metal ring, preferably a semicircular D ring, for attaching the leash or the neck line. Usually this metal ring is sewn in at the buckle end where the collar material overlaps. The main part of the collar is about 1 in. wide and made of heavy leather or heavy webbing. The ends are always made of leather.

Buckle collars can be purchased from sled dog equipment firms or from pet stores. They should be loose around the dog's neck, but just tight enough that they cannot be pulled off over his head.

SEMI–SLIP COLLARS

The best collar for sled dog training and racing is the semi-slip type. The regular semi-slip collar barely goes over the dog dog's head. The adjustable type goes on loosely and then is tightened so that the hand can just go under the collar easily. Both types tighten under tension about 1½ inches so that the collar can neither choke the dog nor come off.

HOW TO MAKE

While sled dog equipment firms sell semi-slip collars or make them to order, they are easy to make at home. All that is needed are two metal rings and webbing. The steel rings are either circular or preferably semi-circular, 1-1/8 in. to 1-1/2 in. maximum outside diameter, of metal which is 1/8 in. to 3/16 in. in diameter. The webbing is 1 in. in width and 3/32 in. to 1/8 in.

COLLARS

Buckle Collar

Stitch Through

Single Loop Nylon Collar

Original adjustable collar by
NORDKYN: P.O. Box 158, Pullman,
Washington 99163

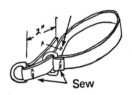

1½" Rings

Use Heavy 1" wide webbing.
Nylon is best.

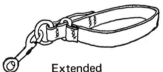

Extended

Under Tension

Semi—Slip Collar

Single Loop Collar Made of Rope

Single Loop Collar
Made of Animal Hide

in thickness if of nylon or 1/8 in. to 5/32 in. if of cotton. Cotton is not as strong or durable as nylon and is slower to dry. The webbing must be firm enough so that it does not twist in use. Thinner webbing can be used if it is sewn into double thickness.

The thread to use is critical, but many types are satisfactory. Waxed linen thread can be obtained at shoe stores. Dental floss is adequate. Non-twist nylon fishing line is excellent. Do not use cotton. Very strong needles such as upholstery needles are required. Most collars are sewn by hand unless a heavy upholstery-type sewing machine is available.

Steps to making a semi-slip collar:

1) Seal one end of the webbing: burn if nylon, stitch over the end if cotton.

2) Run this end through both rings and overlap two inches of webbing. (see diagram)
Caution: Don't make the loop so long that when the collar is pulled tight your dog can reach the extended end with his teeth and chew it.

3) Sew the end, creating a loop with both rings in it.

4) Sew one ring at the end of the loop.

5) Measure where to sew the other end of the collar onto the other ring by placing your collar around your dog's neck.
When pulled tight, the collar should just fit the neck behind the ears. It should not pinch or bury itself in the skin.

6) Cut and seal the end of the webbing.

7) Sew the other end around the loose ring.

Identification plates may be pop-riveted onto the webbing. Identification tags dangling from the ring get lost too easily.

FULL SLIP COLLARS

Never use a full obedience training slip collar made of chain or any other material except in special training situations such as when a leader is being trained with the handler on foot. The danger of using any type of full slip collar, except when a person is on the other end of the leash, is that the owner will either let the dog loose with the collar still on or will tie him up with it on. Too many dogs have been strangled to death because a thoughtless owner left the full slip collar on when the dog was unattended. Hooking the snap on the leash to both rings of the collar is purely a stopgap measure because then undoubtedly the collar will be too big and can come off over the dog's head.

Full slip collars are especially dangerous in a dog team because the dog may become involved in a tangle of such intensity that he cannot be freed before he has been choked to death. Full slip collars are illegal in all sled dog races, as are chain collars of any kind.

SINGLE LOOP COLLARS

Sled dog collars can be made of a single loop, but they are not as satisfactory as the semi-slip or the buckle collar. However, they have the advantages of being low cost, since rings are not required, and easy to make.

Natives of the far north make single loop collars out of a thick strip of tough animal hide like walrus. A ½ in. x ¼ in. strip is slit at one end and the other end pulled through and knotted. The snap fits over any part of the collar except the knot.

Similarly, drivers with 3/8 in. polyethylene rope make simple, cheap collars by eye-splicing both ends. The snap goes over any part of the collar.

If one splice is made so that it has a 2 in. long eye, this type collar becomes a semi-slip collar. The snap goes through the long eye.

HARNESSES

A sled dog must have a properly fitting harness to transmit its forward pull to the line attached to the sled. Different types of harnesses are used for speed racing and for weight pulling or freight hauling. Speed racing sled dogs pull comparatively little weight individually, so their harnesses can transmit the pull from their chest along or across their back. However, sled dogs pulling a heavy load, whether by themselves or as a team, must have the power transmitted back from their chests without downward or sideward pressure on their hind ends.

SPEED RACING HARNESSES
BELLY BAND HARNESS

The simplest racing harness has a horizontal padded chest strap held in place by an adjustable neck strap and an adjustable belly band. While relatively easy to make and fit, the adjustable buckles can irritate a dog with a thin coat. However, this harness has the advantage of not pulling off over the dog's head if he balks or turns around. It is a good basic harness for beginners.

SIWASH HARNESS

The harness most used by modern racing drivers is the Siwash harness, developed by North American Indians for fast trapline runs. It consists of a padded neck loop with a vertical, padded chest strap. No buckles are used, so the harness is not adjustable.

If you fit each dog's harness individually, that is fine. But be prepared for your dogs to change in size and shape from year to year and even throughout the year. Each dog may eventually have several harnesses, or one harness will be switched from dog to dog.

Owners of large kennels make or order their harnesses by small, medium, large and extra large. They know which size each dog takes. The same size may fit a small dog who is stocky and a large dog who is rangy. The size, not the name of the dog, is marked permanently in a conspicuous spot on the harness.

LEATHER COLLAR HARNESS

A type of harness no longer in racing use but of historic interest is the leather horse collar style. It was extremely popular in the early days of the All-Alaska Sweepstakes. The harness is completely made of leather with a padded leather collar being its main feature. To distribute the pull evenly, the two side straps are attached to a hard leather curved loop set outside the soft padded leather collar. A belly band, side straps, and a singletree complete the harness. In later years, side straps were replaced by a single back strap as illustrated in the recent photograph. This entire harness weighs about 24 ounces, which is considerably heavier than the modern nylon, 3 ounce Siwash harness.

LEATHER HARNESS
Antique leather collar harness on Tofty, modern Alaskan husky who is too small for this harness and who does not understand what it is all about. (Photo by Bob Levorsen)

FREIGHT AND WEIGHT PULL HARNESSES
BUCKLE TYPE
The buckle type harness is easily adjusted and is a good beginner's harness. The buckles can irritate a dog with a thin coat, however.

SIWASH
The Siwash type is more popular with modern freight and weight haulers, but is more difficult to fit.

BUYING A HARNESS
Harnesses are available from quite a few sled dog equipment firms throughout North America. Ask your local mushers or watch club newsletters and the trade journals for advertisements. Some firms make harnesses to your dog's specific measurements, and others have them made up by stock size. Either way, it is wiser to send the measurements of your dog on a first order so that the firm can tell which of its sizes will fit best. Measure from the breast bone to the highest point of the shoulder behind the neck, from that point to the base of the tail, and the circumference around the chest. Pull the tape measure tight.

The prices of harnesses vary, but they should be somewhere between eight to twelve dollars each.

MAKING YOUR OWN HARNESS
Many sled dog owners make their own harnesses. It is probably best to buy or borrow a new or used harness and then try to work from the model.

RACING HARNESS
Webbing
A harness takes about four yards of one inch wide webbing. You can find suitable webbing in army surplus or hardware stores. Sometimes it can be found in a tent and awning type store.

You want a soft webbing that will not irritate the dog. You also want one that will not stretch completely out of shape

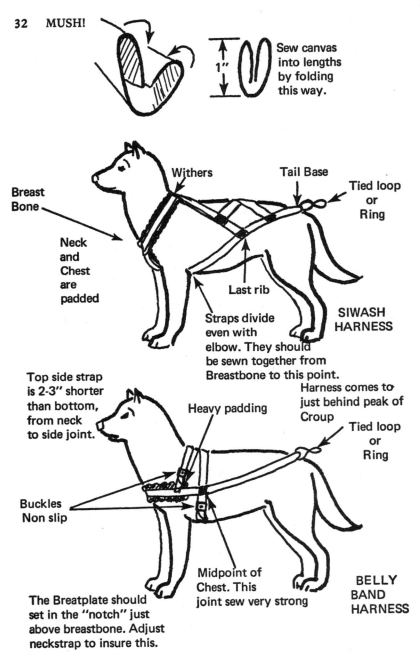

Sew canvas into lengths by folding this way.

1"

Withers

Tail Base

Tied loop or Ring

Breast Bone

Neck and Chest are padded

Last rib

Straps divide even with elbow. They should be sewn together from Breastbone to this point.

SIWASH HARNESS

Top side strap is 2-3" shorter than bottom, from neck to side joint.

Heavy padding

Harness comes to just behind peak of Croup

Tied loop or Ring

Buckles Non slip

Midpoint of Chest. This joint sew very strong

BELLY BAND HARNESS

The Breatplate should set in the "notch" just above breastbone. Adjust neckstrap to insure this.

RACING HARNESSES

or shrink too much when wet. It is best always to wash material before cutting in order to prevent shrinking later.

Nylon is the recommended webbing because it is strong, durable, will stretch slightly under tension but recover when the strain is released, will dry quickly, and is easy to sew. Some types will shrink appreciably. The plastic upholstery webbing used for outdoor furniture is not suitable because it is too hard. Cotton webbing is satisfactory, but it will shrink and takes a long time to dry. Leather is not recommended because it will stretch out of shape when wet, becomes hardened with steady use unless looked after carefully, and the dogs like to chew it. It is also heavy, expensive and hard to sew.

If you cannot find suitable webbing anyplace, use regular canvas folded twice so that no raw edges stick out to ravel. Sew lengthwise on the sewing machine several times.

Padding
Pad the harness as shown with pre-shrunken woolen or fake fur type synthetic material. The padding can be sewn to the webbing by machine.

Fit
It is most important that the harness not choke the dog or pull down across his forelegs to impede his running. Keep experimenting with a harness that is pinned or stapled together until you have it adjusted so that it lies comfortably on the dog both at rest and when he pulls. Ask friends to help "stretch" the dog and trot him on leash with a light load behind, so that you can be sure nothing is cramping his style. Then sew the joints permanently.

Sewing
You will probably have to sew your harness by hand. A coarse weave makes this easier. Washing will often remove sizing and make sewing easier. Use an upholstery needle and the strongest thread you can buy. Shoe stores often have waxed linen thread. Dental floss works adequately. Nylon

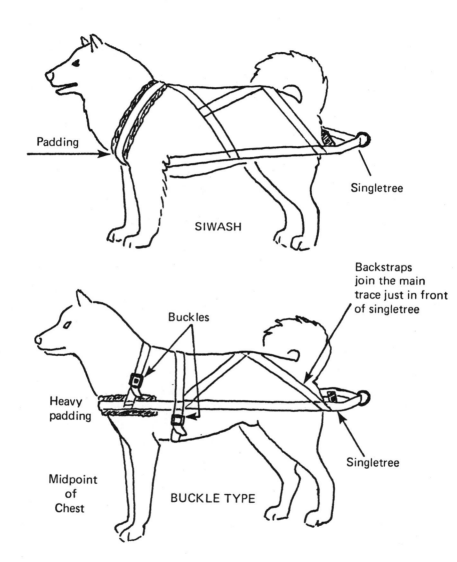

Padding

Singletree

SIWASH

Backstraps
join the main
trace just in front
of singletree

Buckles

Heavy
padding

Singletree

Midpoint
of
Chest

BUCKLE TYPE

FREIGHT HARNESS

fishing line is excellent if you get the type that does not twist. Do not use rivets. They pull out easily and may irritate the dog's skin.

End Loop
The snap from the tugline attaches to a loop added at the end of the harness. The loop can be made of a small diameter, well-spliced polyethylene. Make sure the snap fits over it easily. An easier method is to make the loop of heavy, well-knotted nylon cord.

The length of the loop depends on the length of each individual harness. Adjust the length of the loop so that the harness fits into the gangline. If the loop must be so long that the snap has too much room to slide back and forth, put another splice or extra knot near the end to confine the snap.

WEIGHT PULLING HARNESS
Follow the suggestions about materials, fitting and methods of construction given under Racing Harnesses. The freight harness must have a singletree firmly fastened on either side just behind the dog's buttocks. It should be about 12 to 14 inches long, and can be made of ½ in. or 5/8 in. wooden dowel which is available in any hardware store. Drill a good-sized hole through each end of the dowel. With multiple thicknesses of very strong thread or twine, lash it in place in the harness so that when the dog is "stretched" it sets an inch behind his buttocks — behind the body, not the hair. If you do not use a singletree and your dog pulls strongly, all the fur will wear off his hips. If you put it too far back in the harness, it will hit his legs and make them sore.

Be careful in fitting a freight harness because a bad fit will discourage your dog from pulling the heavy loads you want him to pull.

HOW TO PUT ON A HARNESS
Buckle type harnesses are no problem to put on. The Siwash harness, on the other hand, is often put on either backwards, inside out or incompletely.

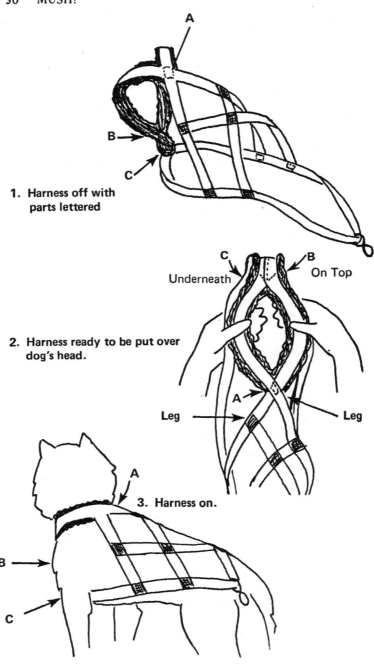

1. Harness off with parts lettered

2. Harness ready to be put over dog's head.

3. Harness on.

When putting on a Siwash harness, hold the dog, sitting or standing, between your legs. Straighten out the harness. Make sure the padding is on the inside. Open the collar and the underarm straps behind the C division at the lower end of the breast strip as shown. You will be holding two pieces in each hand. Now slip the combined collar/straps down over the dog's head. Reach down and lift first one and then the other foreleg over the unpadded underarm straps which are lying across the dog's shoulders. Work the harness back along the dog's body.

If the double center strip ends up down the dog's back instead of down his chest, the harness is upside down. If the padding shows completely and is not partially covered by the webbing, the harness is inside out. If the harness does not lie smoothly, check to make sure you have brought each leg through its proper opening.

HOW TO TAKE OFF A HARNESS

Reverse the process of putting on the harness. Slide the back part of the harness up to the shoulders. Bend each foot up, one at a time, almost double and cover the dewclaw with your hand so it won't catch. Lift it through the strap. When both feet are out, pull the harness back over the head.

LINES

LINE SYSTEMS

A variety of line systems have been used to connect sled dogs to the sled.

FAN HITCH

In the far north beyond the tree line where trails are often blown over by the constant winds, the fan hitch is used. It is so called because each dog's harness is connected by a line directly to the sled and the dogs spread out in a fan shaped array. The leader has a longer line and so keeps out in front. The younger dogs have the shortest lines to give them other dogs to follow and to keep them close to the driver.

While this system has the advantage of spreading weight when going over thin ice, it is somewhat inefficient on solid footing since only the leader and one or two other dogs can pull directly ahead. Also, dog fights are harder to prevent since the leader has no control over the dogs behind him.

SINGLE FILE

In heavily forested areas, a single-file system evolved which is still in use today in Scandinavia. It requires lines on both sides of each dog extending from the leader to the sled. Bamboo poles are used instead of lines in Norway. This system is practical only with small teams.

DOUBLE FILE

The paired dog system is in almost universal use elsewhere today, although dogs that are run singly are often spaced among the pairs. This tandem hitch system requires a central towline with separate tuglines extending outward to each dog's harness. In addition, a neckline extends from the towline to each dog's collar. The entire combination of lines is called a gangline.

HOOKUPS — DOUBLE FILE SYSTEM

Sections of lines are combined to suit the number of dogs being run. All towlines need a single or double leader line in front. To increase the size of the line to accomodate more dogs, add 2—dog sections. However, large team drivers do not build up their gangline from only 2—dog sections. They will have 8 and 10—dog sections plus several 4 and 6—dog sections.

If a single dog is to be run in a space provided for two dogs, attach both tuglines to his harness and, if not a leader, both necklines to his collar.

With all hookups, check the distance between your wheel dogs and your brush bow. If the distance is too great, the sled won't corner well. However, if it is too short, the brush bow will hit the dogs too easily when the line slackens a little. A general rule of thumb is that there should be just space enough for one of your own dogs to fit between your wheel dogs and the sled. If you do not have enough space in your hookup, add an extender to your towline between the gangline and the bridle. An extender is a separate length of towline with a loop at each end.

BUYING A GANGLINE

Most purchased ganglines are made of plastic rope, but increasing use is being made of vinyl coated galvanized steel aircraft cable. Plastic rope is cheaper, but the dogs cannot chew through the aircraft cable. Ask your local musher for suppliers or watch for advertisements.

MAKING YOUR OWN GANGLINE

TUGLINES

Tuglines are generally made from ¼ in. polyethylene (plastic) diamond-braid rope. This material is available at marine and other hardware stores. If unavailable in your area, you can

**TYPICAL
3 DOG
HOOK UP**

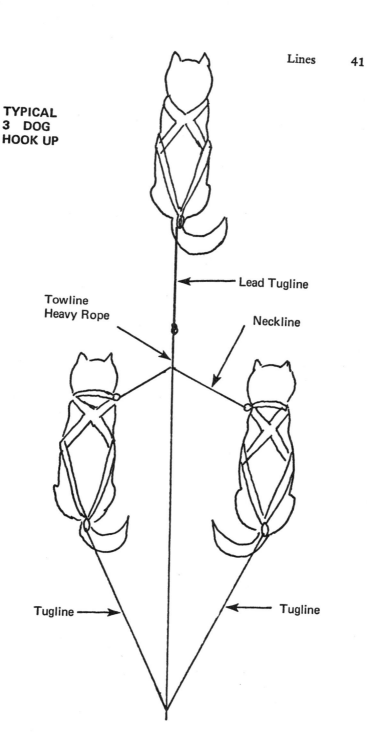

Lead Tugline

Towline
Heavy Rope

Neckline

Tugline

Tugline

substitute diamond-braid nylon rope. If you live in the far north, you can use strips of walrus hide. Diamond-braid rope is preferred over twisted rope because it is easier to splice.

Two-dog tuglines for attaching directly to the sled bridle or for use as a double leader line are generally made in a Y shape, although two single-dog lines can be used.

NECKLINES

Necklines are usually made of the same material as that used for the tugline and are spliced into the towline.

Before the days of snaps, and in some cases even today, large loops were used instead of snaps at the end of the neckline. The loop was put on by pushing it under the collar before sliding it over the dog's head. The loop doesn't freeze the way a snap will, but it takes longer to unfasten than a snap.

DOUBLE LEADER NECKLINES

Double leaders are usually coupled together with a separate double neckline. These necklines are also handy for holding a dog in the basket of the sled, hanging up harnesses, and making a variety of emergency repairs on the gangline. Large team drivers always carry an extra one with them on a run.

TOWLINES

The central towline takes more strain than the tuglines so is made of heavier material. Generally 3/8 in. polyethylene, diamond-braid rope is used.

To prevent larger ganglines from tangling during storage, sometimes small loops of string are added to the towline to which the tugline snaps are fastened. Keep these loops small so that there is little chance of anything getting caught in them, and keep them easily breakable in case something does get caught.

SHOCK CORD (RUBBER COVERED WITH FABRIC)

Shock cord is often added to the line system to ease the strain on the dogs when there is a sudden stop. Sometimes shock cord is sewn inside a tug or towline. However, position-

LINES

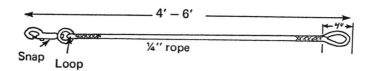

ONE DOG OR SINGLE LEADER

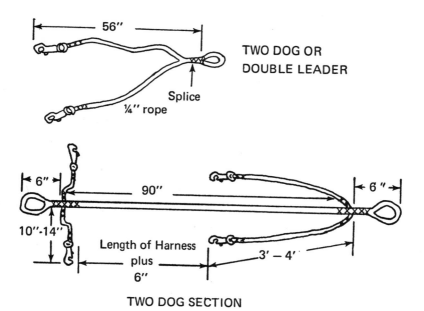

TWO DOG OR
DOUBLE LEADER

TWO DOG SECTION

ing the shock cord in the tug or towline presents two problems, First, the shock cord shortens the line with a permanent bulge, so this shortening must be allowed for when the line is first measured. Second, the shock cord can cause unnecessary trouble with tangles. If a dog has a line looped around its leg, any easing of tension on a normal line will cause the line to fall to the ground and the dog can untangle himself. If the line has shock cord in it, it must be eased much more before it is loose enough so that the dog can free himself.

Most mushers add their shock cord to the bridle of the sled or put it in a towline extender immediately in front of the bridle.

FASTENINGS

Toggles

To fasten the tugline to the harness, some Alaskan natives and others attach a simple toggle to the tugline. The wooden toggle will not freeze, is cheap, but can break unless made of strong hardwood.

Snaps

Tugline snaps are always of the bolt type. Spring snaps can work loose and are usually neither strong enough nor quick enough to release. All snaps must have a swivel to prevent the line from twisting. Snaps can be made of either steel or brass and are about three inches long. Steel snaps are the strongest but need to be oiled frequently, and even so, they will freeze up. Warming them in your ungloved hand will usually thaw them quickly, as will blowing on them in a gloved hand. However, your lips or tongue can freeze to the steel snap, so be careful.

Neckline snaps are also of the bolt type and have a swivel. They are made of brass if possible to lessen the chance of the dog's tongue freezing to them. The nick caused by a dog's tongue freezing to the snap is not only painful but it leads to bloody splatters which freeze all over the dog's face and throat, causing the spectators to think that the dog has been horribly wounded.

TUGLINES FASTENED FOR STORAGE

Figure 8 Knot
(before tightening)   Harness Loop

TOGGLE TUGLINE   Toggle

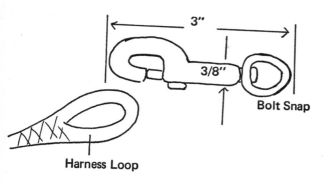

3"

3/8"

Bolt Snap

Harness Loop

Tugline Loop

PASS LOOP THROUGH EYE, THEN OVER END, THEN SNUG DOWN.

Neckline snaps vary in length from 2 in. to 3 in. with diameters of 3/32 in. to ½ in. and should weigh only an ounce or so, about half as much as your tugline snaps.

Since snaps need to be replaced when they break or the spring wears out, they should not be permanently spliced into the line. Instead, splice a loop into the end of the line and loop it over the snap as shown.

Attaching Loops

Attach two loops to each other by pulling one through the other as shown. Since several lines and snaps must be pulled through the loop, make your loops big enough to accommodate everything that must pass through them. A big loop lessens frustration when you are in a hurry.

**Method of Fastening Two
Loops Together.**

SPLICING DIAMOND–BRAID ROPE
Fids

When you buy your ¼ in. and 3/8 in. polyethylene, diamond-braid rope, be sure to purchase also a plastic fid to fit each size rope. The fid fits over the end of the rope and assists greatly in weaving the rope into loop and other splices.

Loop Splices

The basic splice for ganglines is the loop splice. First, seal the end of your plastic rope by melting it with a match. Smooth the melted plastic as it solidifies so that there are no bumps. Next, place the fid over the end of the rope as far as it will go. Force the fid through the rope where you want your splice to start.

SPLICING

Fid   Rope

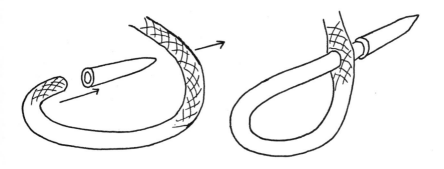

START SPLICING

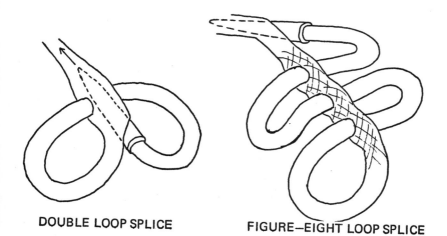

DOUBLE LOOP SPLICE   FIGURE—EIGHT LOOP SPLICE

For the *double loop splice,* circle the fid back and insert it into the center of the rope, through the section making the loop, and then down the main part of the rope. For the *figure-eight loop splice,* weave the fid back and forth a few times before pushing it down inside the center of the main rope. In both splices, hold the original loop at its proper size while the fid is pulled tight. How far the line extends inside the center of the main rope depends on the amount of strain that will be put on the particular loop. The fid is then pulled out, leaving the end of the rope inside.

The double loop splice cannot pull out. The figure-eight splice will not pull out if the end inside the rope is at least four inches long. However, to be absolutely sure, sew the splice into place at its end with heavy waxed thread, nylon line, or dental floss.

Splicing to the Towline

Necklines and tuglines are spliced to the towline by any method that involves looping the line through itself and the towline. The method illustrated makes a neat splice which cannot pull out or slip.

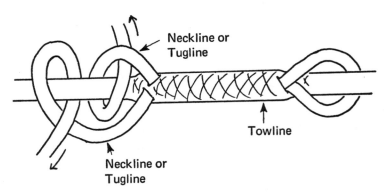

NECKLINE OR TUGLINE SPLICE BEFORE TIGHTENING

TESTING THE GANGLINE

After making your line, hook your dogs up and check carefully how the dogs fit into it. Pairs of dogs should run with heads side by side. Make sure the neckline attached to the towline angles back to the dog's collar, not forward to it. You do not want the dog stretched out tightly, but if the neckline is behind his head, the dog is apt to step over it. To make different sized dogs fit the line, adjust the loops on the rear of their harnesses rather than change the length of the tug. You must allow yourself freedom to move the dogs from one position to another.

If the line from the harness pulls down too much over the wheel dogs' rears, your line is too short. Add an extension to your towline or to the sled's bridle to lessen the angle.

FASTENING THE GANGLINE TO THE SLED OR CHASSIS

Attach the gangline by pulling it through the loop on the bridle of the sled or chassis as shown in the illustration *Method of Fastening Two Loops Together.* Or you can add any of a variety of strong and secure metal snaps or shackles to the loop of the bridle and fasten the loop on the gangline directly to it, with no pulling through necessary. The main advantage of a metal fastener is that in case of emergency, the sled or chassis can be changed while the dogs are still hooked in the line.

TRAINING CARTS, CHASSIS or WHEELED RIGS

A wheeled vehicle of some type is necessary if you live in an area with not enough snow cover for a long enough period to allow you to train your dogs properly with a sled. Wheeled rig races are run from the New York City area to California and even in Alaska in early fall.

CART RACE
Gabi Decker followed by Robyn Murer, Santa Rosa, California
(Photo by Ed Murer)

LIGHT CARTS
DESIGN

Most carts for small teams have three wheels and are designed so that the driver stands. It is much easier to correct a team from a standing position when much hopping on and off the cart must be done. These rigs seldom are built alike, so examine as many of them as you possibly can before you decide how to build yours. Then don't worry if yours looks different from all the others.

WEIGHT

Considerable weight is desirable, not hampering. An adult husky can easily pull a 100 pound rig on level, firm going with the driver riding. Lighter rigs are hard to control and often do not stop readily even with the brakes locked as the dogs can skid the wheels. However, the rig should not be so heavy that the dogs get discouraged trying to pull it. They must be able to go fast when you want them to. If you ever want to go slower to build up their muscles, drag a tire.

BALANCE

The rear wheels must be located far enough apart to maintain stability.

The standing area must be close enough to the axle to keep the front wheel from raising. Don't count on your dogs to hold it down. The front wheel rises easily when going over bumps.

FRAME

For the frame itself, probably the best choice is either steel pipe, extruded angle or channel, or heavy metal tubing. While the pipe joints may have threaded connections, welding is preferable.

Wooden or aluminum frames don't hold up long enough to be worth building.

REAR WHEELS

Large wheels of at least 10 in. diameter are essential. The minimum standard is the heavy wheelbarrow type. Other types that have proven to be good are: go-cart or golf-cart, small trail bike, farm implement, small automobile, boat trailer, and certain types of airplane wheels. Pneumatic tires are more satisfactory than solid rubber.

FRONT WHEEL

Note that the front wheel is smaller than the rear ones. There are several pivoting methods that may be employed in the design of the front wheel. Certain types of heavy duty, ball bearing, swiveling caster wheels will work — with minor alterations. Another method is to use a wheel hub from a small vehicle, or a piece of solid rod working inside a close fitting pipe. Regardless of the swivel method used, the axle for the front wheel should trail the swivel point by a 15 to 20 degree angle.

BRAKES

The type of braking system used will depend on the type of wheels that are used. The easiest to fabricate, and the most popular is a paddle which rubs against each wheel. The paddle can be a piece of 3/16 in. flat iron bent to the diameter of the tire, a piece of 1-½ in. pipe, or a piece of rebar. The paddle for each wheel is connected by a piece of pipe, or solid rod stock, running across the width of the cart. A spring holds the paddles away from the wheels until they are activated by a foot lever attached to the pipe or rod.

Small automobile wheels, along with some golf-cart and go-cart wheels, have the advantage of a drum braking principle.

An emergency or locking brake is useful. However, unless the cart is over 150 pounds, even two or three dogs would have little trouble pulling it with locked brakes. An easily contrived locking system involves attaching a sliding lever to the deck in front of the brake pedal. While the pedal is held down with one foot, the lever is engaged by the other foot.

STEERING

Steering is recommended to help avoid rocks and other obstacles and to make it safer to go around corners. Since carts are much more dangerous to dogs than sleds in a passing situation, steering is required in the ISDRA Cart Race Rules.

For a three-wheeled cart, a yoke extended above and to both sides of the front wheel provides leverage points for lines to be attached. Either two lines or one continuous line can be attached to the handle bar. Greater turning radius is attained by crossing the lines in front of the handle bar.

BASKET

A floor for your chassis is necessary to carry a passenger or a dog. It can be made of either plywood or heavy wire. Wire gives more with the bumps, but plywood gives better protection when you go through a mud puddle.

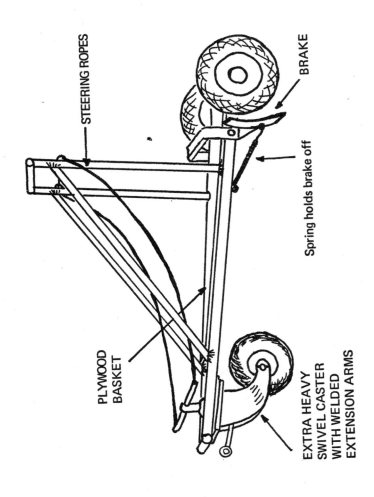

SAFETY FEATURES
Weld a deflecting guard in front of the rear wheels or paddle brakes to keep any object from getting caught in the wheels.

Avoid unnecessary projections.

All sharp edges and corners should be ground off.

BRIDLE FOR TOWLINE
Weld a ring or a piece of flat iron with a hole to a suitable area on the forks of the front wheel. It is recommended to hook to the forks rather than the chassis because the front wheel directs the travel of the cart. The cart will stay directly behind the team and not wander. Also, the front wheel will not spin or chatter when bumps are hit.

If desired, a permanent heavy polyethylene loop can be attached to the hole or ring to prevent wear on the line.

LIGHT CART
Foot bar operates internal braking system. Rope under handle controls steering. Weight 150 pounds. (Photo by Bob Levorsen)

MEDIUM CARTS

Drivers training 5 or more dogs at a time must have a cart with brakes that can be locked if necessary and that weighs so much that locking the brakes prevents the team from dragging it very far, if at all. Three wheeled carts weighing between 200 and 350 pounds are popular. There are several commercial manufacturers. Often used carts of this weight are for sale, and there are a few three and four wheeled vehicles that can be converted, such as golf carts.

HEAVY CARTS

For training 10-12 dogs at a time, a converted automobile chassis used to be the only kind of vehicle available. However, many 4 wheeled all-terrain-vehicles (ATVs) are now available and are commonly used. These ATVs can be easily carried on a small trailer. They have a motor which can be used to help a team up a steep hill, and they can be backed up slowly if a leader starts to take the wrong trail.

WORKING CARS

Because of the danger of overrunning the team, cars or trucks requiring engine power all the time are rarely used during training, except with large strings of dogs, or when there needs to be more passenger room in the vehicle. However, when away from home and between race sites, training using the dog truck can save a lot of time finding and checking out suitable snow trails allowing the use of a sled.

AUTO CHASSIS
Early fall training in Alaska. Driver, Bill Sturdevant; leader, Tuffy.
(Photo by Bob Levorsen)

RISDON RIG
This medium cart has 13" rear tires
with locking hydraulic brakes
(Photo by Bob Levorsen)

ALL TERRAIN VEHICLE (ATV)
Mike Boaz of Truckee, California,
with his 4-wheeled ATV
(Photo by Bob Levorsen)

DOG SLEDS

For winter traveling on snow and ice, a dog sled is used. Basically it consists of two long runners, a frame that holds them in position, and a brake for slowing and stopping the team.

Racing sleds have evolved from the heavier freight sleds of the early days, incorporating their best features but eliminating much of their weight and adding certain refinements. The best racing sleds are beautiful examples of expert wood craftsmanship.

BEGINNER'S SLED

A beginner does not need a proper sled to enjoy having his dogs pull him on the snow. Anything that will not fall apart, has at least 1½ in. wide runners so that the sled won't sink into the snow, has a handle bar to hang onto, and has a brake capable of holding the team will do nicely. Old skis make satisfactory runners for this kind of sled. While a makeshift sled is fine for the period during which the beginner is deciding whether or not he wishes to take up this sport seriously, a regular sled will enable his dogs to perform better if he ever decides to race.

BUYING A SLED

When the time comes that you want a proper sled, it is strongly suggested that you buy a new or used one because unless you are an experienced woodworker with all the equipment for bending runners, making your own sled is a difficult job.

New sleds come in a variety of styles and prices and are available from several sled builders in North America. Children's sleds and those that are bolted together are the cheapest and may be just what you need for your purposes. The regular racing sleds have tied joints for flexibility and do not come apart as readily as the bolted ones. Tied sleds range in price from $400.00 and up plus shipping. New sleds are often hand crafted to order, so be prepared to wait several months for delivery.

Used sleds are fine if you can find one for sale.

For names and addresses of new sled builders, and possibly anyone having a second hand sled for sale, ask your local mushers. Also watch for advertisements in club newsletters and the trade journals.

MAKING A SLED
DESIGN

The most important features are lightness, strength and good braking power. A certain amount of flexibility makes the sled easier to ride and keeps it from breaking apart. Too much flexibility can make it difficult to control.

The critical parts of the sled that take the strain are marked in the diagram with a star.

MATERIALS FOR FRAME

Use ash, oak, birch or maple. Metal tubing has been used, but is not satisfactory as it is almost impossible to incorporate the required amount of flexibility.

WEIGHT

An average sled weighs about 30 pounds. A much heavier sled does not have any more stability than the one of average weight. A much lighter one can be difficult to control and is apt to be of such thin construction that it will break up easily.

Cut to length all the pieces of wood you plan to use and weigh them. If they weigh too much they are too thick and need paring down.

MEASUREMENTS

For an average dog sled the approximate measurements are:
Width — center to center of runners: 19½ in.
Width of runners: 1-3/4 in.
Thickness of runner: 5/8 in. at front tapering to 1 in. in the

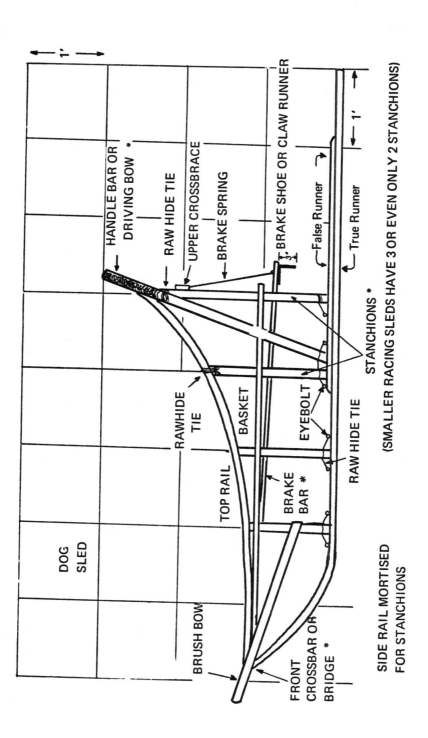

DOG SLED

HANDLE BAR OR DRIVING BOW *
RAW HIDE TIE
UPPER CROSSBRACE
BRAKE SPRING
BRAKE SHOE OR CLAW RUNNER
False Runner
True Runner

RAWHIDE TIE
BASKET
TOP RAIL
BRAKE BAR *
EYEBOLT
RAW HIDE TIE
STANCHIONS *

BRUSH BOW
FRONT CROSSBAR OR BRIDGE *

SIDE RAIL MORTISED FOR STANCHIONS

(SMALLER RACING SLEDS HAVE 3 OR EVEN ONLY 2 STANCHIONS)

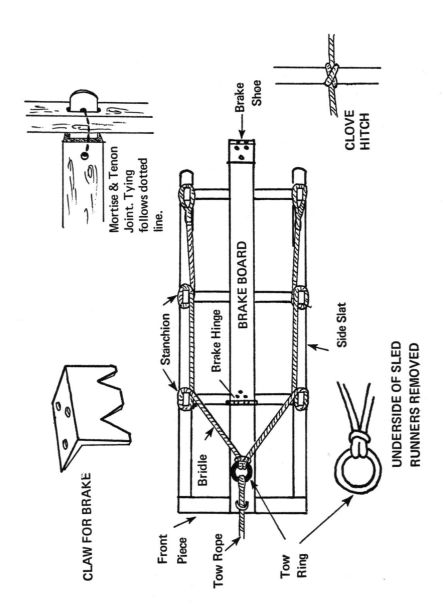

Mortise & Tenon Joint. Tying follows dotted line.

CLAW FOR BRAKE

CLOVE HITCH

Brake Shoe

BRAKE BOARD

Stanchion

Brake Hinge

Side Slat

Bridle

Front Piece

Tow Rope

Tow Ring

UNDERSIDE OF SLED RUNNERS REMOVED

middle and rear
Length of runners: 7½ ft. total
Height of basket: 10 in.
Height of handle bar: 32 in.
Crossbars: 7/8 in. x 1¼ in.
Stanchions: 7/8 in. x 1¼ in.
Length of basket from front crossbar to rear crossbar: 4 ft.
Length of runner behind basket (where driver stands): 3 ft.
Brake board: 5/8 in. x 3½ in. x necessary length.

BRAKE

The brake board is bolted to one of the forward crossbars of the sled with a heavy, gate type hinge. The free end at the rear is suspended from the upper crossbrace by a length of shock cord (strands of rubber bundled together inside a woven fabric sheath) or by two screen door springs. Fasten the shock cord or springs to the brake in such a way as to not interfere with the foot which must use the brake. Sometimes a wide boot gets stuck between springs that are too close together and too close to the end of the brake.

The brake claw is often made from a piece of heavy angle iron of about 3 in. or 4 in. on each side. Cut off a length equal to the width of your brake board. The claw portion should be cut out with a hacksaw. The other side is drilled and bolted onto the brake board.

FASTENINGS

A good racing sled is held together mainly with mortise and tenon joints which are tied with heavy nylon cord (3/16 in.) or with rawhide (¼ in.). Use a good quality rawhide obtainable from a leather store, not the half-cured material on sale for boot laces. Ask your dealer which kind of leather would be best suited to your purposes.

Cut a continuous strip around your piece of leather about ¼ in. wide. Soak it overnight in water before using it. Tie as securely as possible. The leather will contract and tighten as it dries. One word of caution about using rawhide on a sled: Never thoughtlessly tie an unattended dog for a long period where he can reach the sled. He is apt to make a meal out of the leather.

MOODY SLED
Sled made in New Hampshire by Ed Moody. (Photo by Bob Levorsen)

A sled may be entirely bolted together if it is not expected to receive strenuous use. But if it is pulled too fast over too many miles of rough trail, the bolts will work loose and/or the wood may crack.

Most sleds do have a strong bolt on each side where the runner meets the forward crossbar. Make sure this crossbar is strong.

Eye bolts are secured into the runners on both sides of every stanchion to take the rawhide or nylon ties. The ties run through a hole in the stanchion.

Wood screws or ties are used to fasten the basket slats to the crossbars.

RUNNERS

The true runners must be strong yet lightweight. They must be flexible to get through rough spots and around corners. False runners, placed on top of the true ones, are optional. They are short and for extra strength.

The surface upon which the musher stands is usually made less slippery by the addition of a piece of carpeting, bicycle tire, or even metal which has had nail holes punched through. The carpeting must lie flat, so fills up pretty quickly with snow and becomes icy. The bicycle tire is better because being round and flexible with room for give, the snow build-up can easily be kicked and bounced off. The metal with ragged nail holes is hard on shoes and knees.

In order to prevent damage to the runner bottoms when you hit a rock or bare ground, the runners can be shod with steel. Cold-rolled steel is durable but "sticky" on snow. Stainless steel is faster. Spring steel is the best. The shoes are bolted through the wood of the runner and the false runner with the heads of the bolts thoroughly countersunk into the metal. Steel runners work best at temperatures over about 25 degrees Fahrenheit. At lower temperatures snow, ice and fresh dog droppings freeze to them in lumps with considerable friction resulting.

Racing sleds usually have plastic material fastened to their runners. Several types are available from dog sled equipment firms and sometimes from ski manufacturers. The usual is yellow P-Tex, a high molecular weight polyethylene. This material is lighter and produces less friction than steel on snow and ice. All ski plastics are thin (1/16 in.) and hard to glue to the runners unless they are cloth backed. For glueing, use at least three coats of good contact cement on both the runner and the plastic. Ski plastic is soft and scratches badly on bare ground or stones. It may be easily smoothed and dressed by using a wood plane of the "Surform" type.

ATTLA SLEDS
Made by George in 1967 — Made by George in 1991
(Photos by Rick Meyer & Bob Levorsen)

Other plastics are much tougher than ski plastic and only a little less fast. A good white material — a spaceage, high density polyethylene — is ¼ in. thick and is usually bolted to the runner. Unless many bolts are used, contact cement is necessary between the material and the wood runner to hold them together between bolts.

Dog mushers are forever changing the material on the runners of their sleds either because what is on the sled wears out or they want to use something different. The easy way to do it is through Tim White's "Quick Change Runner System". This system involves screwing aluminum slide rails onto each true runner and then sliding plastic runners onto them. Plastic changes take only 5 minutes so runners more suitable for the snow conditions can be substituted easily before use. Sleds can be bought with slide rails already attached, or the rails can be screwed on almost all sleds that don't already have them. Scraping and waxing of plastic runners is now carried out by almost all competitive mushers so that they can at least start out with the best wax on the best plastic.

BRIDLE

Install a bridle as shown in the diagram. Use a heavier polyethylene rope than that used for your towline. In the middle of your bridle fasten a large and strong metal ring at least 1½ in. diameter, or make a knotted loop. Remember that both your towline and your snowhook fasten to this ring so you need room.

The ring, or loop, goes in the center of the sled approximately under the front crossbar. Carry the ends of the bridle back, attaching them with clove hitches to the stanchions as you go. Use a loop splice around the last stanchion involved. To give the dogs a straight pull all the way, attach the bridle lines to the stanchions just below the basket so that they are as level as possible with your main towline.

The ring or bridle loop must be held approximately in position both vertically and horizontally to keep it from getting caught under the runners and to guide the direction of the sled. Running the main towline through a U bolt attached to the front crossbar accomplishes both objectives at once. Otherwise, the ring can be suspended vertically by a line fastened loosely to the front crossbar and positioned horizontally by lines fastened between the ring and both forward stanchions.

Before taking your dog team out, put a practice tension on your towline and check to make sure everything is working smoothly.

HANDLE BAR

Usually handle bars (sometimes called driving bows) are covered with friction tape or soft leather to make them easier to grab and hang onto. The friction tape is sometimes painted a bright color.

BRUSH BOW

The brush bow's purpose is to deflect the sled from anything it might hit, so it is an important safety feature. It is tied in position. It must be able to "give" a little or it will break easily.

Toboggan Sled photo by Lucy Bettis

TOBOGGAN SLEDS

Toboggan-style sleds have become popular for long distances races and for camping trips. They have a flat smooth bottom just inches above the runner base, providing flotation in deep snow and keeping heavy loads close to the ground.

ANCHORING THE SLED

WHILE HOOKING UP THE TEAM

Sleds are firmly attached to an immovable object while the team is being harnessed and attached to the towline. This prevents the team and sled from running down the trail before the driver is ready. Three methods are commonly employed: the snub rope, the quick-release, and the snow hook.

The *snub rope* usually consists of about 15 ft. of soft, ½ in. diameter rope, It is firmly attached by splice or bowline knot to the loop on the end of the towline or to the iron ring to which the towline is attached. The snub rope is never tied to the sled itself, since that can result in the sled's breaking apart.

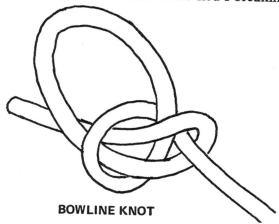

BOWLINE KNOT

The loose end of the snub rope is tied to an immovable object such as a tree or strong post. Use a slip knot and tie it within easy reach of the sled. Watch the knot as you hook up because it may work loose.

It is important that the driver have one hand on the sled handle bar and at least one foot on one runner when he pulls the end of the snub rope and unties the slip knot. If he is not holding on firmly when he unties the knot, the team will start down the trail without him.

After the team takes off, the dragging snub rope is wrapped around the handle bars. If left dragging, it may get under a runner, the driver may step on it, or it may interfere with another team.

The *quick-release* works in a similar manner to the snub rope, but the rope and the metal release remain attached to the other immovable object, which may be the driver's car. The quick-release unsnaps even under extreme pull or tension. It can be purchased at any horse equipment store.

The quick-release rope goes around a solid part of the cart or around the lower part of the rear stanchion of the sled. When the release is pulled, the rope then slides around the stanchion. Since the quick-release must be fastened to the sled, it should not be used with large, powerful teams since the sled could be pulled apart.

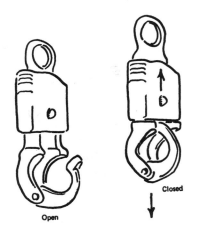

QUICK RELEASE

Snow hooks are frequently used instead of snub ropes or quick releases since most drivers carry one on their sled anyway. The snow hook is hooked around the immovable object and pulled free by the driver when he is ready to go. As with the snub rope, the snow hook rope is attached to the towline (or its iron ring), but never to the sled itself. The driver must be able to free the hook while standing on one sled runner and holding onto the handle bar.

The snow hook does not quick-release. With a strong team, the driver, and perhaps his handler, must pull the sled backwards a few inches to reduce the tension on the hook so it can be pulled free.

WHILE ON THE TRAIL

Every driver must be able to get off his sled to undo a tangle or move a dog from one position to another. While the brake can stop the team, it cannot be used to anchor it, so other devices must be available. Different methods are generally used for sleds and carts.

ANCHORING THE SLED
Snow Hook Angle

Sled snow hooks take many shapes, depending on typical snow and trail conditions to be encountered. All hooks should have an angle of from 55 to 70 degrees. This angle tends to make the hook dig itself deeper into the snow as more forward pull is applied. Although they are easier to build, hooks should never have a 90 degree or right angle, as with this large an angle they pull out of the snow too easily.

Snow Hook Lines

All snow hooks have a line permanently attached to their forward end with a loop at the opposite end big enough for the hook to go through. This makes it easy to attach the hook to the loop at the end of the towline, or to the ring to which the towline is attached. The length of this line is different for each sled, and is determined by the requirement that the hook must be set in the snow next to where the driver stands. The driver must be able to pull the hook free while holding onto the sled handle bar.

Hooks also have a 12 in. to 18 in. line on top of the rear end, so they can be pulled straight up to free them from the snow.

Single Prong Hook

For hard packed trails and trails with trees near enough and small enough to get the hook around, the single-pronged snow hook is best. It sets firmly in the hard snow or around the trees. It may weigh from 2 to 4 pounds for a small team and from 10 to 15 pounds for a large team.

Double Prong Hook

In softer snow conditions, double-pronged hooks are popular, as they provide twice the holding power with only a little more weight.

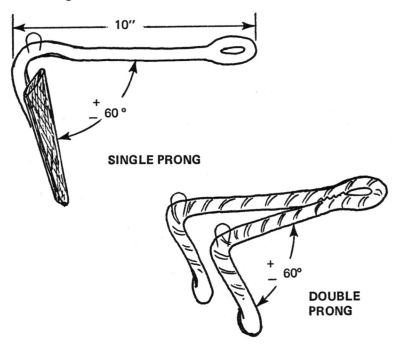

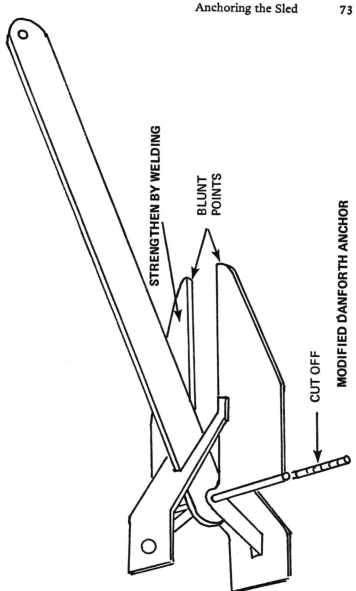

STRENGTHEN BY WELDING

BLUNT POINTS

CUT OFF

MODIFIED DANFORTH ANCHOR

Danforth Anchor

In extremely soft, deep snow, very few snow hooks are satisfactory. One type that will work is a modified 2½ lb. Danforth sailboat anchor, which can be purchased at almost any boat store. This anchor will hold a ½ ton sailboat in soft mud or a 15-dog team in deep powder snow because it digs deeper and deeper as more pull is applied. A rear pull rope of 3 ft. to 5 ft. is required since these anchors will go that far down into the snow. In fact, a knife should be carried to cut them loose in case they can't be broken free.

Setting the Hook

Setting the snow hook is critical. Many drivers have lost their teams because the snow hook would not hold. The proper procedure is as follows:

1. Stop the team with the brake.
2. If a suitable tree or other immovable object is within reach, a) put your hook around it
    b) push the sled forward to tighten the hook line.
3. If no tree is available, a) place the hook, point down, into the snow just outside the runner.
    b) With one foot still on the brake, step on the hook with the other foot. Push it down as far into the snow as you can.
    c) With that foot still on the snow hook, let up on the brake and call or otherwise urge the team forward. The forward movement of the sled will firmly set the hook — if the proper hook is being used for the snow conditions encountered.

Breaking Hook Loose

Breaking the hook free from the snow is much easier than setting it. With both feet on the runners and one hand firmly on the handle bar, just pull up on the short rope at the rear of the hook.

An experienced and well-coordinated driver will sometimes

not set his hook firmly on purpose, even with a large team. After adjusting the team, he will call to the team to pull the hook free. He will not run back to the sled but will wait for it to come to him. To reduce the relative speed of the sled, the driver turns and starts forward, grabbing the handle bar as it goes by. After a few steps, he jumps on the nearest runner.

However, if your snow hook pulls out while you are at the head of your team, you should take no chances. Try to stop the team by grabbing lines or the sled brush bow. If they all go by, belly flop across the sled's basket. Then climb over or around the handle bar onto the runners.

More teams are lost by improper snow hook setting than by losing the sled on hills or curves. As a new driver, you should practice setting the hook on training runs until you have confidence in your ability to make it hold. If the hook won't hold on a training run, get a bigger or better designed one before going out again.

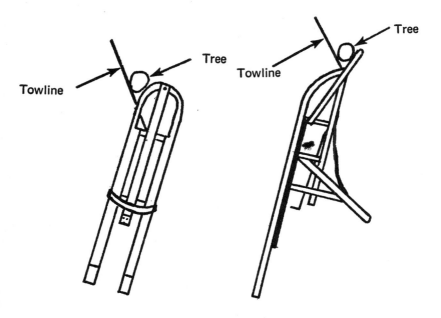

ANCHORING WITHOUT A SNOW HOOK

Anchoring Without a Snow Hook

Although it does not involve a snow hook, one way to anchor a team with complete security is to wedge the sled around a tree of the proper size. Turn the sled on its side and push the sled so that the brush bow is on the opposite side of the tree from the towline. The team cannot pull loose unless the sled, line or tree breaks.

Another way to anchor a team without a line is to carry the sled off the trail, turn it on its side, and push it down into the soft snow.

If you are carrying a snub line, the sled can be secured by wrapping and tying the line around a tree or post.

ANCHORING THE TRAINING CART

Carts are more of a problem to anchor than sleds. Some come with built-in emergency brakes which simply keep the brake on. Most teams, however, can drag a small cart, even with the wheels locked, faster than a driver can run. Big team drivers usually use a four-wheel, heavy, car-frame type cart to avoid this problem.

Small cart drivers have utilized two solutions. One is to add to the cart itself a two or three-pronged metal fork which the driver forces into the ground after stopping the team. On hard ground this type attachment usually causes the rear wheels to lift off the ground when set.

The other solution is to attach a sharp, double-pointed snow hook to the cart. It is set in soft ground as it is in hard snow. On hard ground, pulling the cart sideways and resting one wheel *on* the double-pointed hook helps.

Turning the cart on its side helps with a small and tired team. A strong team that wants to go can pull it along with them and it probably will bounce back on its wheels.

Many drivers avoid the cart hook problem by training with teams too small to cause serious problems if the cart can't be anchored. This still results in useful exercise.

CARRYING A DOG
IN THE SLED

Dogs do not like to ride in the sled even when they are too tired to run. The bouncing and jostling will agitate the dogs, and they will do their best to get out. While some dogs will run off and get lost if they manage to get loose, most will stay just out of reach and either lead or follow the team home. A loose dog that cannot be caught will automatically disqualify a team in a race and may interfere with other teams, so drivers do their best to keep them in the basket.

The simplest method of securing a dog in a sled is to fasten two double necklines to the sled and snap one to the dog's collar and one to the rear of his harness. The dog is always faced backwards so he can be controlled by the driver's free hand. The lower the dog is kept, the less likely he is to capsize the sled with his weight shifts. Carrying two dogs in the sled at one time is often necessary in a long race and can be quite a feat.

SLED MAT

To prevent the feet of a carried dog from slipping between the slats of the basket of the sled, the basket is usually covered with a sled mat. Most mats are made of heavy canvas with grommets in the corners. The corners are tied to the sled with nylon string. Strong nylon netting can be fastened or woven between the side rails and the basket, and across the back to keep dogs and gear from falling out.

DOG BAGS

A dog bag is simply a device for enclosing a dog while he is being carried to keep him completely under control. A dog bag will help keep an injured dog from further injury, but unless the bag is well designed, any dog who has any strength left will fight being put into one. The dog is put in backwards with his head sticking out towards the rear of the sled.

Heavy canvas or plastic cloth bags with zippered or draw string openings are the most popular. Most dog bags are firmly attached to the sled before the run, and serve as a floor mat.

If ISDRA race rules are being used, dog bags are required. If not, the race entry form should say whether or not dog bags are required.

Dog bags may be purchased from most of the sled dog equipment firms, or they may be made at home.

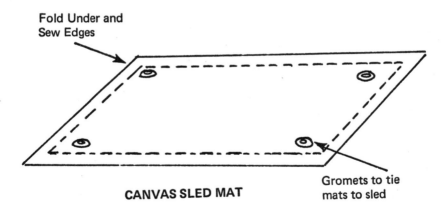

Fold Under and
Sew Edges

CANVAS SLED MAT

Gromets to tie
mats to sled

ACCESSORIES

SLED BAGS

Canvas bags with tie-on strings are almost always carried on the sled. Though usually tied onto both rear stanchions, there is less windage if the bag is tied to one side.

Some of the items carried in the bag are:

        Snow hook
        Spare gloves and hat
        Double neckline
        Extra harness
        Noise makers (rattle, etc.)

Instead of putting the snow hook in the bag, some drivers put their hook under shock cord fastened over their sled mat or in a plastic holder secured to a rear stanchion.

Sled bags can be purchased or made at home.

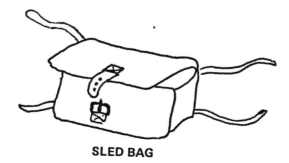

SLED BAG

DOG COAT

Thin coated and older dogs may need protection from extreme cold before and after running. Sometimes a coat is put on a dog who is apt to get stiff, just as a blanket is put on a race horse.

Blankets can be made of any heavy material that is preshrunk.

The pattern shown is easy to make. "A" fits across the nape of the dog's neck. Lap "B" and "C" over each other in double thickness. Fasten with anything, even two safety pins. If you make the neck opening large enough to go over the dog's head, you may sew "B" and "C" permanently together. Tape "D" should be long enough to have the ends cross under the dog's belly and tie on top of his back.

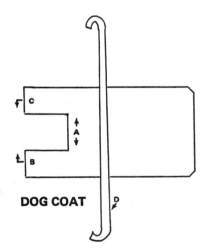

DOG COAT

DOG BOOTS

Dog boots can be helpful during long distance traveling where icy trail conditions exist to prevent feet from getting cut. They will also protect feet already damaged. However, they wear out quickly and care must be taken when tying or taping them on. If fastened too loosely, they will fall off; if fastened too tightly, they can impair circulation.

Exceptionally bad weather conditions during the 1974 Iditarod Trail race caused a tremendous number of emergency dog boots to be needed. The Anchorage *Daily News* printed an appeal for boots, and in two days 4,500 were donated. The *Daily News'* instructions were:

"Making the dog boots is simple. They can be made of heavy canvas or mattress ticking cut into a 'U' pattern seven inches high and four inches across. Once the simple 'U' pattern is cut, all that needs to be done is to sew a zig-zag stitch around the 'U' and put a hem at the open top of the 'U'." (Anchorage *Daily News,* March 9, 1974.)

Boots made of various materials are widely available through suppliers and are inexpensive. Velcro fasteners make them easy to put on and take off.

TRAILS

Always know what you are getting yourself and your dogs into when you go out on a trail. Either go over a new trail yourself first, or get a detailed description from another dog musher who has been over it.

TRAIL LAYOUT

Sled dogs must have some sort of a road or trail to follow. Unfortunately they cannot be taken to a place like a large field or frozen lake and just told to go. They won't know where to go.

Basically the team should always go forward. So the ideal trail is a big loop. Variations on the complete loop trail are ones that go out for a certain distance, split to go around a loop, and then join the original trail to come home. Depending on the size of the loop at the end, these are sometimes called lollipop or needle trails. No matter how small the loop is, there should be one.

If at all possible, avoid stopping a team in the middle of a trail, turning it around manually, and then returning back over the same trail. This practice may teach the dogs that they can stop at a certain distance, or, worse yet, whenever they feel like it, turn around and come home.

You can use a one way trail if you can arrange to have someone pick you and your dogs up at the other end.

As much as dogs like to go out, they like to come home better. They have a sense of direction and memory that enables them to know when they are headed home. Therefore, avoid a trail that comes back to, or near to, where the team

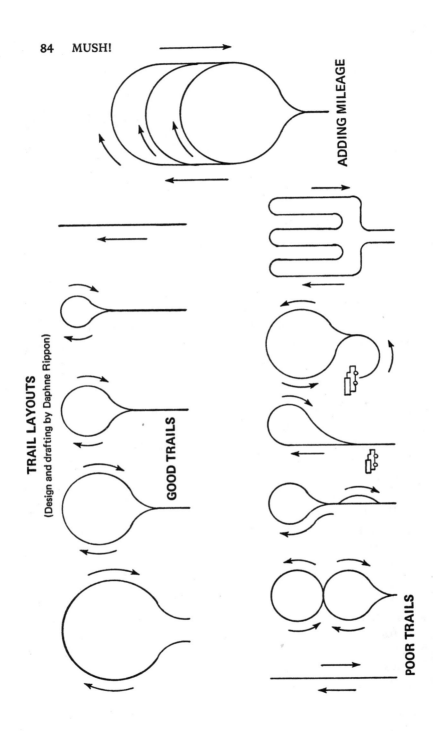

ADDING MILEAGE

TRAIL LAYOUTS
(Design and drafting by Daphne Rippon)

GOOD TRAILS

POOR TRAILS

has started and then keeps on going — such as going around a race track more than one time.

Also, avoid having the team either cross the trail it came out on, or come back on that trail for any distance at all, and then veer off to take a different way home. The dogs know which trail they came out on; they know where their truck is; they will be most upset if they are not allowed to follow the "home trail" all the way home.

Special trails for lead dog training will be discussed in a different section.

Avoid a trail that at any time before it comes into the home stretch gives the dogs a good view of their own truck, or similar vehicles, or the starting area — and an opportunity to cut to it. This is particularly true at the beginning of a run. If the dogs don't go directly away from their truck and starting area, there will be trouble.

Also avoid a going-out trail and a coming-back trail that are so close to each other that the dogs can easily cut from one to the other. Depending on the barrier between them, the trails shouldn't be any closer than 50 or 60 feet apart. Also avoid a trail that winds back and forth on itself with "fingers" so close together that the dogs can either cut across or become confused as to whether they are going out or coming back. "Finger" trails have too often been put in when someone is trying to get the most mileage — or spectator viewing — out of a large meadow or frozen lake.

Also avoid trails that could be hazardous to yourself or your dogs. Hazards include hills that are so steep and/or long that you can't slow the team down to a safe speed; adjacent banks that your sled or cart might go over; too many rocks, trees, ditches, or sharp curves that could cause you to lose the sled; highway crossings; any places where your team could cut from your intended trail to run down a well traveled or paved road. If at any time you might tangle with too much automobile traffic, take someone along with you to help.

Obviously, suitable trails are hard to find. Some people who live in rural areas can make their own. Others living in more populated areas may have to travel many miles. When you do find, or make, a good trail, stick to it. The dogs won't become bored quickly, and in the beginning both you and the dogs gain confidence from knowing where you are going. Soon the dogs will need a longer trail anyhow. When that time comes, either find a new trail or try to add mileage to the one you are using. Add mileage by adding an extra loop which avoids all the pitfalls mentioned above.

TRAIL SURFACE
FROZEN SURFACE
Hard packed snow makes the best running surface for a sled dog. The dogs seem to enjoy it most of all, and it is easy on their feet. A light dusting of snow on top of the hard packed trail is fine, too, because it gives under the feet and doesn't interfere with running.

Punchy snow, the kind with a hard crust on top but soft snow underneath, isn't good. The dogs' feet break through the surface at odd intervals. The dogs can sink down from a few inches to clear out of sight. This is discouraging and tiring to the dog that breaks through and to the other dogs who have to help drag him out. At the very least, it breaks the rhythm of the whole team.

Deep snow is tiring to the dogs, too, but at least it doesn't take them by surprise the way punchy snow does. Ordinarily if the snow is too deep for good running, mushers will pack the training or race trail with some sort of tracked vehicle before taking the dogs out. If a team unexpectedly finds itself in snow so deep that the dogs bog down and cannot get through, the musher must walk in front of the lead dog to break trail for him. In areas where this kind of deep snow is expected, the experienced musher takes snowshoes on the sled with him.

Corn snow is a deceptive kind of surface. This condition occurs when the snow forms in little round pellets which are not noticeable at first. This type of snow is abrasive, and dogs who must run on it for any distance will get sore feet.

Jagged ice crystals, formed by snow that has melted and

frozen again, make the worst kind of frozen surface to run on. Smooth ice is all right if gone over slowly, but broken ice will cut the dogs' feet and is to be avoided at all costs.

WATER

If the weather is very cold, avoid going through any water such as overflow on a frozen river or lake. The dogs' feet will freeze if wet. Should the team go through water by accident, stop immediately and dry the dogs' feet with snow. Sled dogs, as a rule, usually don't like water no matter what the weather. Possibly, this dislike comes from an old instinct which tells them that getting wet means freezing to death.

DIRT

A dirt road or wide path is fine for running dogs on a chassis. A little rounded gravel doesn't seem to bother the dogs' feet too much because it gives. Too much gravel for too long a time will raise a blister on the pads which is hard to detect. Sharp gravel is to be avoided because it will cut the dogs' feet.

One problem with dirt roads is that they become muddy when it rains. A few water puddles don't bother the dogs at all — some dogs go around them and some plow right through. But deep mud sticks to the chassis wheels and the dogs' feet and can make the going pretty hard, sometimes impossible. These conditions are discouraging to dogs and musher alike and should be avoided if possible.

PAVEMENT

Pavement is all right in the beginning if you are just jogging with your dog on lead. After the dog starts to dig in and pull, the pavement will take the pads off his feet in an amazingly short distance. For this reason, cart races are never held on pavement.

If your trail crosses a paved road, slow the team down before you go over it and the dogs' feet won't be damaged.

PINE NEEDLES

Pine needles make an excellent running surface. The dogs enjoy running through pine forests, and the needles are smooth and give under the feet. Pine needles make an excellent surface for a drag sled as they are amazingly slippery.

PRECAUTIONS

Check out a new trail from end to end to see what conditions are before you run your team over it. Remove broken glass, tin cans and other debris which will hurt the dogs' feet. You may have to remove some rocks and fallen logs or fill in gullies. Mushers spend a lot of time working on their trails.

If you run your dogs on a road that has been commercially cleared of snow with the help of chemicals, be sure to clean your dogs' feet with fresh snow when you come back. The chemicals used to melt the snow can be poisonous if licked and introduced into the dog's digestive system.

If an otherwise good trail has a few bad spots of various kinds here and there, don't worry. Just slow down when you come to them. Dogs get much less foot damage when going slowly.

AGE TO TRAIN

Research by behavioralists Clarence Pfaffenberger and John Paul Scott has proved that a dog is most receptive to new ideas between the ages of three weeks and three months. Scott says that the puppy has an adult brain at seven weeks, and that he will never forget what he has learned between the fourth and sixteenth week.

It is better to teach the puppy desirable traits during this receptive period than to leave him alone and let him pick up undesirable ones. The desirable traits that the puppy learns now will socialize and stabilize him and will be the basis for formal training later on. They will also be the basis for making him a satisfactory pet.

However, most people start their sled dog racing careers not with a young puppy but with a grown dog. Any suitably built dog up to the age of about eight years can be trained with varying degrees of success to be a sled dog. The degree of success depends on the physical condition and mental attitude of the particular dog and on the skill and patience of the trainer.

Sled dogs are considered to be in their prime from about four to six years. But they have frequently been run on competitive teams from 6 months to 12 or 13 years.

In 1973 George Attla had a 13 year old leader, Blue, when he came in fourth in the first running of the 1,049 mile Iditarod race from Anchorage to Nome. Another female, Tex, was 10 years old when she was on loan as a leader on George Attla's winning 1972 speed race team, and was 12 when she ran double lead with 11 year old Nugget on Carl Huntington's winning 1974 Iditarod race team. In 1975, Nugget, now age 12, again won the Iditarod, this time as leader for Emmitt Peter's team. Blue, Tex and Nugget all were retired after their long races — and later presented their surprised owners with puppies.

Whatever the age of your dog, adapt the training instructions to suit his previous experience.

PETER
Ready for training at 6 weeks.
(Photo by Rick Meyer)

TRAINING SCHEDULE

How often you train your dogs depends on how much time you have, what stage of training your team is in, and what degree of proficiency you wish your team to attain.

In the beginning, when you are jogging with your dog on a leash near your home or are going a short distance on a cart or sled, it is best to take the dogs out four or five times a week. You want to train them often enough so that they remember what they are learning, but don't train them so often or so hard that you put so much pressure on them that training ceases to be fun. If this happens, they will start to act bored or look for ways to get out of what you want them to do. Even though you don't think you are putting too much pressure on the dogs, try always to think of it from the dogs' point of view: what THEY think is too much pressure.

If the dogs do become bored or act up, reduce the number of weekly training sessions for awhile. Their mental attitude is more important than the number of times you take them out. If you diagnose their problem as insecurity or fear, continue to take them out as often as before, but make the lessons shorter. Increase the fun of the outing by showing more enthusiasm yourself and by playing with them afterwards.

As your team advances in training, becomes stronger physically, and goes a farther distance, three times a week can be enough to run if that is all you can manage. If your situation is such that you can run only on weekends, those two days a week will get results, but not as much as if you could run more often.

Drivers ordinarily do not run too many days in a row because the dogs become tired anu bored. But running two days and then resting for a day or two is good because most races are two-day affairs. The dogs might as well learn they must run two successive days.

For a yearly schedule, established drivers usually start training in the fall as soon as it gets cold enough. The younger dogs need more "miles" than the older ones to get in condition. Training intensifies, with the dogs running about four times a week and with increased mileage, until the racing season starts in January. When the dogs start racing, training sessions are cut in number and intensity. If the team is in condition, it is just kept at that level. George Attla says that when he is racing hard on weekends, he runs only twice during the week. (George Attla, *Everything I Know About Training and Racing Sled Dogs,* Arner Publications, Rome, New York, 1974, p. 61.)

If during the winter you are not racing the dogs hard but are just going out on easy pleasure jaunts, then you can run the dogs for as many days in a row as you wish and they will enjoy it. (Attla, op. cit. p. 146 and Iditarod chapter.)

After the racing season is over in the spring, the dogs who have been running all winter get a rest while the new crop of pups is brought out for training. When it gets too warm, only the lightest training is done with the pups. Do not train when it is hot, like above 60 — 70 degrees.

Traditionally, dogs are not run on a year-round basis— either training or racing. They and the driver need a prolonged rest to store up enthusiasm for next season's running. If the dogs do not get this rest and are run for too long a time, on a yearly basis, they become what mushers call "sour". However, if a driver is in a position during the summer to let his dogs run loose for short periods in a fenced field or under otherwise safe conditions, he will find it beneficial to do so. The dogs love it, and they will stay in better physical condition than if they are kept tied all the time.

If you are starting a young pup, of course you must start training him at the proper age, no matter what time of year it is. And if you are starting with a new dog, also start at any time of the year. After your dogs are trained, then you can go on the seasonal sequence of building up training in the fall, running hard in the winter, tapering off in the spring, and rest in the summer.

SUMMER GOOF OFF
The same Peter several years later;
a reliable, hard working wheel dog.

WEATHER

Weather is an important factor when running dogs. On a clear, cold day, the dogs feel like running and will put out their best effort. But when the weather is too warm, or it is pouring rain, or there is a howling blizzard, the dogs would much rather (and probably should) stay holed up at home.

Just *when* the temperature is too warm depends on where you live, what the dogs are used to, and how thick their coats are. If you lived in the middle of Alaska or northern Canada and the temperature in January got up to 35 degrees above zero, the dogs would think it was too warm to run. If you lived in southern California and it ever got down to 35 degrees, the dogs would be raring to go.

Running in temperatures that are too warm for the dogs can be dangerous. Dogs have a fur coat and do not sweat the way humans do. They let off excess heat mainly by panting. So when the temperature builds up too much they can easily die of heat prostration. And too many have.

Danger from too much heat is not confined to when running the dogs. They have been known to die while being exhibited in a summer parade and even while tied up in their own yard where there is no shade.

At the other end of the scale, running dogs in temperatures that are too cold can also be dangerous. George Attla says in his book that when it gets to be colder than 30 below zero, he doesn't take his dogs out on a training run. If it is 30 below, he will take them out but will go slowly and for only five or six miles. On the other hand, he says that if you have to take the dogs out to hunt food, you don't stay inside no matter how cold it is. (Attla, op. cit. p. 144.)

The danger is that the dogs can freeze their undersides where there is little fur protection. In the old days, mushers used rabbit skin covers for their dogs when forced to travel in such extreme temperatures. (Kenneth Ungermann, *The Race to Nome,* Harper & Row, New York 1963, p. 82.) Dogs can also frost their lungs when breathing too heavily in such cold weather, although this is rare.

To protect dogs from getting overheated when you want to run them in warm weather, it helps to wet them down with water before the run. During a training run, every mile or so, stop the team and offer each dog a drink of water. In a race, if it is REALLY warm and the Race Marshal does not stop the race, it is much more sensible for you to scratch.

Any dog that comes in unusually hot from any run should be wet down. If a dog ever becomes actually overcome with heat - eyes seem glassy; dog stands stiffly or falls down; dog is obviously in distress - then wet his whole body completely down to the skin as quickly as possible. Every minute counts. Don't waste time trying to take his body temperature. If a pond is handy, submerge him and go in with him to hold him. After he is cooled, keep him quiet and do not run him for several days. If he gets heat prostration again, take him to your veterinarian.

ILLNESS and MENTAL ATTITUDE

Your dogs should be trained only when they are in the peak of health. If for any reason they are not feeling well, they cannot give you their best performance. The trick is for you to be able to differentiate between their not feeling well physically and their being mentally out of sorts—or just lazy.

If any dog all of a sudden does not run as well as he has been running, check for something physical first. Start with an examination for sore or cut feet. Check his temperature. Watch to see if he is eating eagerly, or is vomiting, or has diarrhea. Try to think of anything physical that could be wrong with him.

If you can't come up with anything physical, then consider his mental attitude. Have you been asking too much of him? Have you been trying to make a lead dog out of him when he would be happier back in the team? Have you been running him too many days in a row? Did you take him over the same trail twice or more in the same day? Did you hook him up with a dog that he doesn't know, or doesn't like, or is afraid of? Was dirt or snow being kicked up excessively in his face? Are any dogs around in season? These are but a few examples of things that could have been wrong.

Keep in mind that the learning process for a beginning dog is not a smooth progression, but fluctuates, first up, then down a little, then up again. When dogs first start training they are usually enthusiastic because it is something new and they have their owner's complete attention. Then somewhere along the line this training ceases to be fun and becomes work. They become bored. They go into a slump. Perhaps this is just a natural slump period for your dog.

If you cannot come up with any specific physical or other reason for your dog's not doing well and you think this is just a slump period, tie him up for a few days. If you have other dogs, take them out for their training runs and leave him home. This ought to do it. If it doesn't, take him out and work with him gently for a few days, or even weeks, with lots of praise and enthusiasm on your part to try to bring him out of it.

If you have found something physically wrong with him like a cut foot, consider taking him along to the training site so that he can watch the other dogs in action. He can and will learn by observing. Give him some extra attention, like a short walk on a leash, so that he will not feel that he is being punished by not being allowed to run.

Females in season can be run, and run they are, even in the most important races. Just be alert to prevent unwanted breedings both on the trail and around the truck. Put something on the female to mask her own odor. Vicks chest rub, citronella, and feminine deodorant spray are all good. Be careful that no fights occur between males. If you have a female in season and are training with other teams, it is only considerate to advise them of the situation. You would appreciate the same courtesy from them. If you should have a breeding, don't try to separate "locked" dogs, as it is physically impossible. They will separate themselves when they are good and ready.

GOOD ATTITUDE
Laurie Leach tries to keep Ganja under control in the starting chute of the North Lake Tahoe race   (Photographer, unknown)

COMMANDS

WHAT TO SAY

The common commands in sled dog racing are:

To go: A sharp whistle, or, if the driver can't whistle, a sharp sounding word like 'HIKE!' or 'GET–UP!' 'MUSH!' the traditional command in literature is never used, the title of this book not withstanding, because the 'sh' is too soft a sound. The word comes from 'Marche!' the familiar imperative form of the French verb Marcher, to walk. (Virginia Daloyan, Alaska Native Language Center, University of Alaska, personal communication.) It was no doubt the command used in the old days by the French voyageurs when they drove their dog teams in Canada.

Right turn: 'GEE!' with a soft G as in jelly.

Left turn: 'HAW!'

Straight ahead: 'STRAIGHT AHEAD!' 'AHEAD!' 'ON BY'

Speed up: Another whistle, 'GET UP!' clapping hands, slapping something against the sled, rattling a jingler, a kissing sound, etc.

Move a little to one side or the other: 'GEE OVER!' or 'HAW OVER!'

Come: 'GEE COME!' or 'HAW COME!' – Sometimes 'COME GEE!' or 'COME HAW!'

Slow down: 'EASY'

Stop: 'WHOA' delivered in a low tone of voice and drawn out.

Stay in one place: 'STAY!'

Anything wrong: 'NO!' Used either on or off the trail.

Praise: 'GOOD!' or 'GOOD BOY!' Used either on or off the trail. Said with enthusiasm.

All commands should have sounds that are different from each other and different from other words that the dog knows, such as its own name or the names of its kennel mates and names of people in the family. 'Whoa' and 'No!' really sound too much alike, but they are in such common usage that instead of changing the commands, we change the way they are said. 'Whoa' is said low and drawn out; 'No!' is said high and sharp. 'Go!' and 'No!' also sound too much alike, so avoid using 'Go!' for a command to get moving.

Teaching your dogs commands that are totally different from those in common use has a serious disadvantage. If one of your dogs ever changes owners, he will probably have to be completely re-educated in order to fit in with the new team. Or if someone not in your family drives the team, he will probably forget to use the commands that the dogs know.

Commands should be short, either one word or two words that can be run together. The dog must be able to pick the sound out and remember it. Avoid commands like, "Let's get moving there old boy!"

Remember when giving these commands that the dog is learning to associate a specific sound with a specific action. Therefore, use one command and one command only for that specific action. Do not use a variety of commands for the same action. And do not give your command in the middle of a sentence so that the sounds are all run together. The dog must be able to pick out the sound.

Many people, even experienced mushers, have difficulty remembering the difference between 'Gee!' and 'Haw!' It is not unusual to hear a musher who should know better repeatedly give the wrong command to his lead dog — and get increasingly angry when the dog continues to take the command correctly. When the driver suddenly realizes his error, he sheepishly apologizes to his lead dog and wishes he could hide in the nearest snow bank! To prevent making this mistake, some mushers who know they have trouble write G on the right side of their sled and H on the left; or they write the letters on the back of their gloves.

TONE OF VOICE

Margaret Pearsall on page 22 of her book says that voice tones can be divided into four categories: a. Coaxing b. Happy c. Harsh (which she says never to use) d. Demanding. On pages 49 and 50 she says that you should have a happy ring for your praising and authority for your commands. "Let him know you mean business when you demand something. . .A coaxing or pleading voice will not get the desired response." She finishes by saying, "Also, an unusually loud command is unnecessary, as a dog's normal hearing is so acute that it is one of his outstanding attributes." (Reprinted from THE PEARSALL GUIDE TO SUCCESSFUL DOG TRAINING, by Margaret E. Pearsall, Copyright   1973, HOWELL BOOK HOUSE INC., by special permission of the publisher.)

One of the most common mistakes made by beginning sled dog drivers is yelling at their dogs in too loud a voice. Didn't they ever open a bag of cookies in the kitchen when their dog was asleep in another room? Didn't they ever mistakenly rattle a food pan and have their dog come running from the farthest corner of the yard? And yet these same people, when they get on a chassis or sled and have their dogs only 10 or 15 feet in front of them, think they must scream in order to get the dogs' attention.

In the midst of the noise of the starting chute the dogs should hear the command to go. But is this shouting necessary out on the trail where all is silent? These drivers may be relieving their own tensions, but have they considered what it would be like to be in the dogs' place and receive this kind of treatment? Think about it. What happens is that the dogs stop listening. Furthermore, yelling at dogs unnecessarily during a race when another team is close by can be called interference under the International Sled Dog Racing Association rules and can be cause for disqualification.

Use a high and happy tone of voice for your going commands and your praise. Use a low tone and draw out your slowing down commands. Clip off your 'Noes' and 'Gees' and 'Haws' and give them with authority. Say the leader's name to get his attention before giving the turn commands. Always pause between his name and the command to give him time to react to his name before he has to pick out the sound of the command.

Anytime your dog takes a going type command properly, be sure to give him praise immediately afterwards. He must associate the command with the action with the praise and know that he has done the right thing and has pleased you. "Rex!. . .Gee!. . .Good!" Be as enthusiastic as you wish after the going commands, but praise after the slowing down ones might excite the dogs and get them going again.

WHEN TO GIVE COMMANDS

Give a command whenever you want the dog to do a specific action for which you have a command. By far the most important commands for the sled dog are 'No!' and 'Good!' and the turn commands. Teach these to the dog first. The 'No!' and 'Good!' will probably have been picked up as a small puppy, so you should concentrate on the turn commands. Other commands will be picked up as you progress if you are consistent about using them. Don't make any specific efforts to teach the dog all the commands at once.

When you start to teach the turn commands, you should repeat the word several times as the turn is being reached. "Rex!. . .Gee!. . .Gee!. . .Gee!. . .Good!" Although a trained dog should react to one command only, in the beginning he will probably need to hear it several times in order for it to make an impression on his mind.

Be sure to give the command far enough in advance of the turn so that the dog has time to react before the turn is reached. Just how far in advance is this? A good way to find out is to literally put yourself in the dog's place. Jog at a good clip along a trail which is approaching an intersection. Have a friend jog behind you. Have the friend give either turn command, without your knowing which one it will be, and see how long it takes you to figure it out and react properly. Then remember that you are a human who knows the commands well, that you know what is going to happen, and that you are paying close attention. Your dog is supposedly not as smart as you are, he will not be paying as much attention as you are, and he certainly will be going a lot faster. This procedure will give you an idea of when to say the command so that the dog can react properly without breaking his pace.

Of course do not give the command so far in advance of the turn that the dog cannot associate the command with the turn. The timing will depend on how far ahead the dog can see the turn and how quickly this particular dog learns to react.

Once you have given a command and the dog has taken it, give a word of praise and then keep quiet. If the team is doing well, there is no need to say anything. A word of encouragement and reassurance during a long, dull stretch is all right, Even the quiet whistling of a tune is sometimes good to relieve the monotony.

Too often beginners keep talking to their dogs the whole time they are on the trail. They keep urging their dogs to do better when they are already doing their best. This is discouraging to the dogs. The result is that the dogs tune them out as you would a radio that plays all day. Then when the driver really wants their attention to give a command, he can't get it. And the noise escalates. When beginning 3-dog class teams are racing, a checker on the trail can often hear them coming from a mile away. When the top flight drivers are racing, sometimes with a 16-dog team, the only warning of their approach that the checker usually gets is the banging of their sled or the breathing of their dogs.

As well as not talking to your own dogs, also refrain from unnecessary talking with other teams or your own handler who may be riding with you. Before you go out, be sure to instruct any passenger to keep silent when the team is moving. You are the only one to do any talking. People who have never been on a sled before, in their excitement, always seem to chatter away a mile a minute. The dogs are taught to pay attention to everything that is said, and they simply cannot do this if there is a stream of conversation going on behind them. You, the driver, are the only person to do any talking.

TRAINING
THE DRIVER

The novice driver should be aware of the basic guidelines for running a dog team before he actually begins his first run.

Observe experienced and successful drivers in action. You don't have to do everything exactly the way others do it, because your situation may be different from theirs; you may be running fewer dogs, and certainly your dogs will not be as experienced as their dogs, or you may wish to treat your dogs more as pets than they do. Your relationship with your dogs does not have to be changed dramatically just because you decide to run them as a sled dog team. So decide which things they do that would be useful to you and which things would not.

Add to your knowledge by reading as many publications as possible on the subject. Again, some things may be right for you and some may not. You must evaluate what you read—even this book.

Before you take a dog out, take time to think about what you are going to do and how you will go about it. Try to imagine what situations might occur and decide ahead of time what you will do about them.

Similarly, when you come in from a training session, take the time to think about what happened. It is helpful to keep a journal with notes on each run. Record the number of miles covered, which position each dog ran, and how each dog performed. Then try to figure out why each dog did what he did. Think about what you can do differently next time to help each dog who did not perform to your satisfaction. Most things go wrong because a dog does not know what the trainer wants, or because the trainer does not have the dog's attention. You must help the dog to understand what you want. Study your literature again to see if you overlooked some suggestion during the first reading. As George Attla says (*op. cit.* p. 45), "So if a mistake is made in that team, it is you that has made it, not the dog."

One main point in any type of training is to prevent the dog from doing something wrong. Doing something wrong is just as much of a lesson to the dog as doing something right. You can't tell him, "Oh, that was wrong. Let's forget it." He won't forget it. He must unlearn it. As Earnest Barkley, a distinguished dog trainer from New Orleans, always said, "When you let a dog do something wrong, then you have to do it over again right three times: twice to have the dog unlearn it and the third time to teach him the right way."

Therefore, be consistent in having the dog follow your instructions correctly *every* time. When riding a sled or chassis, never hook up so many dogs that you can't stop at any time to correct a dog. If you give your leader a 'Gee!' command, he must go 'Gee'—and nowhere else. You, not the dog, must be in control.

One frequent mistake a beginning driver — and too often an experienced driver — makes is losing his temper. Perhaps nothing has gone right on the job or around the house. You take your dogs out to train them and again nothing goes right. The inclination is to take the whole day's frustrations out on the dogs. This you must never do. Margaret Pearsall on page 22 of her book says, "About the most important thing in the beginning is for you to start to school yourself in your voice control, learning not to show your feelings in your voice, no matter what mood you are in." (Reprinted from THE PEARSALL GUIDE TO SUCCESSFUL DOG TRAINING, by Margaret E. Pearsall, copyright   1973, HOWELL BOOK HOUSE INC., by special permission of the publisher.)

On the same subject George Attla says, "If you could just keep your cool, even when you are mad, if you don't blow up, then you are in good shape. That is one of the main things. If you could just never lose control of your temper. That could run away with you pretty fast. And when you do that, you are goofing up your whole training program. If you want to be a good dog musher, you keep your temper around your dogs." (Attla, *op. cit.,* p. 55.)

Remember that in the dogs' eyes, you are the leader of their pack. Dogs are related to wolves, and in the natural state the wolf pack gives its leader loyalty and respect. To earn this respect, the leader is wise; he is firm, but fair. If you would be a successful leader of your pack and earn your dogs' respect, you also must be what *to them* seems wise, firm and fair. Always think of the situation from the dogs' point of view.

"Scotty" Allan demonstrated this point most graphically in his decisive encounter with Jack McMillan, a dog so undisciplined and vicious that he had once attacked and almost killed a former trainer. Jack McMillan had been whipped constantly, which only made him more defiant. When "Scotty" Allan acquired him, he realized that the dog needed to be conquered in a way that would be more vital but less humiliating than a beating. "Scotty" untied the dog and the two stood facing each other.

"For an instant the man and dog had paused, each seeming to gauge the strength of the other — then the instinct to kill, that heritage from the past, when the timber wolf gave no quarter, rose supreme; and the dog sprang forward, the wide open jaws revealing his sharp, white teeth and the cruelly broken tusks. Suddenly the weight of Allan's body was hurled against him; strong supple fingers closed upon his neck, and with an unexpected wrench Jack McMillan's head was buried in a drift of soft, deep snow. He struggled violently to wrest himself from the iron grasp; madly he fought for freedom, but always there was that slow, deadly tightening at the throat. Panting and choking, he had made one last desperate attempt to break the grip that pinned him down; and then lay spent and inert except for an occasional hoarse gasp, or convulsive movement of his massive frame.

"At length the man had risen, and the dog, feeling himself loosed, and able to get his breath, staggered uncertainly to his feet, turned, and stood bravely facing his foe. . .

"There seemed a sudden comprehension on the part of the

dog, like the clearing of a distorting mist. . .and when "Scotty's" hand fell upon his head, and gently stroked the soft sable muzzle, Jack McMillan had not only met a master, but he had made a friend." (Esther Darling, *Baldy of Nome*, The Penn Publishing Co., Philadelphia, 1923, p. 188.) *

Jack McMillan turned out to be one of "Scotty" Allan's best and most faithful team dogs.

Taking the relationship of you and your pack a step further, it has been demonstrated that the dominant male of the group, the truly alpha male, will in some cases give his respect to a male human much quicker than he will to a female human. The female human will be tolerated, but that is about all. The alpha female dog will accept the authority of humans of either sex much more readily.

A word about your own physical fitness: Don't ever think that dog mushing is a matter of just standing on the sled while your dogs pull you over the snow. While talking about training a beginning lead dog on a leash, Lee Fishback says, "I am not even discussing how you feel by now. Despite the brevity of the sessions, you probably have aching feet, have started on a diet, and are cutting down your smoking." (Lee Fishback, *Training Lead Dogs My Way*, Zima, Kila, Montana, 1974 p. 17.)

George Attla, in his chapter on riding the sled, (*op. cit.*) talks about both pumping and getting off the runners and running to help the dogs out. And he usually has 16 dogs in front of him! You, with your one or three or five dogs, will find that often you must get off and run, particularly uphill. On occasion you will have to wrestle with several strong dogs all at once. And eventually, if you stick with it long enough, you will have to hang on while dragging behind a fast moving sled and manage to pull yourself up on the runners again. The better physical condition you are in, and the less excess weight you are carrying, the easier it is going to be on you — and your dogs.

This chapter would not be complete without some mention of the attitude of the driver toward his sport. The attitude curve for beginning drivers the country over seems to go something like this: The first year of running they know that both they and their dogs are beginners, so they don't expect too much. They are happy just to get around the course without trouble. The second or third year they start taking racing seriously, think they know what it is all about, have bought an expensive dog or two, and are sure they are going to win everything in sight. They get frightfully intense. When things don't work out the way they expect, they get most upset and often take it out on their dogs, other drivers, officials, and particularly their families. About the fourth or fifth year, they come to realize that you don't get to the top of this sport overnight, and they start to relax. They still want to do well and try their best, but it isn't the end of the world when they don't win. As George Attla says (*op. cit.*, p. 165), "Any time a man can get everything his dogs have got, whether they won the race or came in 15th out of 20 teams, this man should be a happy man."

No matter what the circumstances, sled dog driving is always a sport; and there is always more to learn. In the words of one driver, "At the end of every season I always say that I wish I had known at the beginning of the season what I know now — and I have been driving dogs for 15 years."

* All efforts to contact the person holding the rights to this book were unsuccessful. Ed.

BELLA LEVORSEN
Running Alaskan village dogs and a registered English Dalmatian at Hobart Mills in the California Sierra   Tweeter and Heather in lead.
(Photo by "Mally" Hilands)

PUPPY TRAINING

Taken from "Do You Train or Break Your Dogs" by Harris Dunlap, published in the Spring, 1973 INFO, quarterly publication of the International Sled Dog Racing Association. Mr. Dunlap was an ISDRA Director, an outstanding editor of INFO for several years, and he has won many major races. Mr. Dunlap has reviewed this chapter for the 1980 edition.

TRAINING BY WEEKS
THREE TO FOUR WEEKS

According to John Paul Scott's *Animal Behavior* and Clarence Pfaffenberger's *The New Knowledge of Dog Behavior*, the best age to start instilling your puppy with desired associations and behavior patterns is three to four weeks. Therefore, if you have a litter of new puppies, start at three weeks to handle them daily for at least five minutes. Play with the pups and coax them to come to you. Place the bitch, tied, but puppies loose, near the normal flow of family traffic so that the pups will be within easy reach of people. All members of the household, and strangers, too, should handle the puppies. Call them "Puppy, Puppy" so that they associate something you say with something pleasant. This is the very beginning of teaching commands.

FOUR TO FIVE WEEKS

Give each puppy a name and have any person who handles a pup repeat the name while he is playing with him. Still refer to the group as "Puppy, Puppy". This handling and playing will teach each puppy to have confidence in you. The pups will soon wag their tails when you appear and follow you around. They will learn to become socialized with all humans. If you are conscientious about this daily contact, and if you leave the puppies with their mother until the end of the seventh or beginning of the eighth week, you will have well adjusted and emotionally stable puppies.

Scott says that what the puppy learns from the fourth week until the sixteenth week he will never forget. Thus it is important that he learn only good habits at this time. No one needs bad habits that the pup has learned during this time cropping up later.

SIX WEEKS

At six weeks, during the play period, put a harness on one pup at a time and let him play with it on. Occasionally put a string on the end and let the other pups pull on it.

You may wish to put small collars on the pups at this time.

SEVEN WEEKS

About every other day attach a light block of wood to the string. Attach another line to either the front part of the harness or, if the pup has a collar, attach it to the collar. This is a play session. Let the pups lead you around as much as you lead them around.

The session must be fun. Never force any pup to the point of frustration. And never, never strike him. No dog should ever associate pain with training.

(For a training schedule at this age, Thom Ainsworth adds, "Five minutes on, ten minutes off, five minutes on, twice a day. And that's all.")

EIGHT TO NINE WEEKS

Take the bitch away from the litter at eight weeks.

During the daily play-training session, *carry* the pups one at a time a short distance away from their usual play area. Most will run back on their own, dragging the block of wood. If one seems confused, run back to the play area in front of him and coax him to follow. If he stops to investigate some new sight or smell along the route, stop and wait for him to satisfy his curiosity.

When a pup seems stable, take off the block and daily *lead* and coax him away from his home area.

Little by little expose each pup to as many different sights, sounds, smells, and running surfaces as possible. Give him time to explore and smell the new things if he wishes. You are there to give him confidence. If he takes too long with his exploration, coax him to continue his journey. Soon he should be breezing down the road with you running behind hanging on to the end of the harness line for dear life.

TEN TO TWELVE WEEKS

Separate each pup from his litter mates at 10 weeks. The pups will not be lonely because each one will still be getting his usual daily training-play session. This daily attention from you, now with no more play with the other pups, will strengthen the communication between you even more.

Separating the pups at this time will establish each one's self-importance and individualism. If left together, the group would start to sort out its pecking order. Some would learn to be dominant and some subordinate. Some might even start to be bullies. None of these traits is desirable in a sled dog.

COMMANDS

From the third week when you start calling the group "Puppy, Puppy" you are teaching each dog, by association, to respond to words. Shortly afterwards when you give each pup a name and start calling him by it when you hold him, you are doing the same thing.

From the fourth week start saying 'No!' every time the pup does something you don't like. While you are saying it, either push him away gently but firmly, or pull him away by the leash.

When guiding any dog by a leash, do it with a series of small jerk actions rather than a single big dragging motion. If you snap your wrist rather than bend your elbow you will get the desired result. However, if the dog becomes frightened, panics or hangs back, stop the jerking and instead use a steady but firm pull accompanied by a reassuring tone of voice. This is the standard procedure used by all good obedience and other dog handlers.

From the fourth week also start teaching 'Good!' by saying the word whenever the pup does something properly. Put enthusiasm in your voice. It is most important that the pup understands when he has pleased you.

When the pup starts running in harness, start saying 'Hike!' − or whatever your 'Go' command will be − every time the pup takes off after a stop.

At the same stage of training start saying 'Whoa' every time he stops. Create a few extra stop and go situations to reinforce these commands.

All of the above activities should be done in a play-training atmosphere.

PRELIMINARY LEAD DOG TRAINING − 12 to 16 Weeks

At the age of 12 weeks − usually not before − preliminary lead dog training can be started with any pup who has learned to:

1) Respond to the above commands
2) Run in front of you with assurance along familiar trails
3) Cope with confidence with new situations as they arise
4) Drag a block of wood without concern

To start your lead dog training, select an area of tall grass. Mow a grid of paths that cross like a four way road crossing.

Run your future lead dog in front of you down a trail. As he approaches a crossing, step off the trail to the right, pull the line to the right, and say 'Gee!' If necessary make the right turn yourself. Keep pulling or jerking gently on the line and repeating 'Gee!' As the pup starts to make a move in the proper direction, say 'Good!'

Do only 'Gee' turns until the pup understands the command. When he does, then start 'Haw' turns.

Teach 'Ahead' by at first giving the command several times while the pup is running down a straight stretch. Eventually give the command when he is approaching a crossing.

If at any time the pup makes a mistake, stop him and at the

same time say 'No!' Repeat the proper command while pulling and jerking on the line in the right direction. Move in the proper direction yourself. Don't forget the 'Good!' when the pup goes the right way, even if you have maneuvered him there yourself.

RESULTS

If you follow this 3 to 16 weeks' routine faithfully from the beginning, by the time you hook all of your pups up as a team you will have a happy, well-adjusted, and confident group of dogs who know only good habits. No bad habits will be there to overcome. No frightened, tangled, bolting six-month-old beginners will have to be coped with. You will have a trained team — maybe even some leaders — and all by the 16th week.

Mr. Dunlap kindly gave Mush! this follow-up to his article.

Between the 16th week (four months) and the time that the puppies are physically mature enough to be hitched in a team and pull a sled (usually six to eight months), they are put on a schedule of daily socialization. They are played with, taken for walks on a leash, and taken along in the dog truck when the older dogs in the team go someplace. They are not just left on the chain and ignored. But further practice on the drag during this time does not seem to bring significant results.

The six to eight month variation in age for the time of the first hook-up depends on the stage of maturity of the individual dog. Although none will be completely mature, some will be more mature than others. The variation in time also allows the first hook-up to take place during good weather and at a time of year when the owner is not completely occupied with the older dogs.

For the first runs, pick a level trail with good footing. If the pups are trained well enough on the flat, they will be able to handle hills with no trouble later on.

Take the pups out in teams of from three to five dogs, depending on the experience of the driver. A beginner can take two pups and one leader. An experienced driver can take three pups and two trained leaders or two pups and three leaders, depending on how enthusiastic the pups are. After five or six runs, more pups can be used together because they will settle down.

Nothing special is required for the first runs except that everything must go smoothly. It is the first time the pups have worked together as a unit, and whatever happens will make a great impression on their minds. The pups must never be asked to stand still while being hooked up and there must be no pain whatsoever involved.

The preliminary training should be sufficient to have the dogs run without trouble once they get going. If any problem develops, it may be because the pups got their preliminary training on snow and are now running on dirt with a chassis, or the other way around. With patience, the dogs should adjust after a few runs.

The distance to run depends on the humidity and the heat. In the summer the runs should not be more than 1½ miles, and with frequent stops. The number of times the pups are taken out is more important than how far they go. Five 10 minute sessions get better results than one 50 minute run. But take the dogs out at least once or twice a week at this stage.

During these runs rotate the positions in which the dogs are hooked. Some dogs have a preference for one side or the other, just as people are right or left handed. Others are ambidextrous.

After eight months, continue the socialization process by exposing the pups to new sights and sounds. Take them to the store or shopping center and stake them out around your truck. Take the shy ones for a walk on a leash around the area. Do as much working on a one to one basis with the pups as you have time for.

Bring each pup into the house on occasion, perhaps even once a day. (Mr. Dunlap is speaking of kennel dogs. Ed.) A dog does not have to be kept on a chain all his life to get him to work. Don't keep him in the house for so long a time, though, that his system becomes adjusted to too much warmth.

In summary, good sled dogs are the result of:
1)   Good breeding
2)   Good health, nutrition and conditioning
3)   The response to sound

In the long run, the dog that is taught to respond to a happy sound like a whistle will turn in a better performance than one that is driven by a pain-fear mechanism. And there are good physiological reasons to support this observation.

BOB LEVORSEN
Running Alaskan Indian Dogs at Hobart Mills in the California Sierra
with Knik and Peggy in lead   (Photo by "Mally" Hilands)

ADULT
DOG TRAINING

This section is a step-by-step discussion of how to proceed with an untrained dog, from taking him out of a vehicle to having him run smoothly in a team.

The instructions assume that the owner is starting out with one or more adult dogs who are physically mature enough to pull — about six months old — and who have never had any training. Every dog is different and will react in a different manner, so not all situations can be covered. Only typical reactions and the methods to cope with them have been given. Adapt the instructions to suit your dog, your training area, the people with whom you are training, and the time you have available.

Make every effort to do your training with other beginners or with an established team. It is good for your morale and good for your dogs to be around other people doing the same thing. At any stage of beginning training, it will help you to watch experienced dogs handled by an experienced driver. And it will help your dogs to watch an experienced team in action.

You may be able to contact the sled dog club nearest you by inquiring from the owners of northern breeds. Watch newspapers for announcements of local races.

SETTING UP
TAKING DOG OUT OF VEHICLE
When taking a dog out of a vehicle, don't let him jump from a height of more than two or three feet as he might strain his shoulders when he lands. Instead, hold his collar with one hand and as he comes out of the vehicle, support him with

the other hand under his chest. Many dogs will jump out with such vigor that the owner is knocked over backwards if he is caught unprepared.

WALKING WITH THE DOG
If the dog is too strong to be walked with all four feet on the ground, lift him by the collar to a vertical position and let him hop along on his hind feet. This position does not hurt the dog, and he is much safer than if he pulls you off your feet and gets loose. It is wise for you to practice this maneuver before the dog gets too strong and before you must accomplish it on icy footing.

SECURING DOG TO TRUCK
If you must travel to an area beyond your own property to train your dog, don't let him run loose if other people or dogs are around. Keep him on a leash or snap him to a chain attached to your vehicle. The dog must be given time to relieve himself before training starts. It is wise right from the beginning to learn your dog's elimination habits. A dog which has not relieved himself sufficiently shortly before a run will often cause a delay during the run. The dog may either stop suddenly, or he may just not run well. So watch your dog while he is on the chain to see whether or not he performs; and when he does, pick up the droppings immediately. Any training area should always be kept as clean as possible. If a dog is not used to being tied and won't perform, take him for a walk on a long leash. This may have to be done before reaching the training site.

A dog also needs a little time on the chain to look over the new area and any new dogs and people who are there. The sight of other dogs should increase his enthusiasm for the run. Give him a little time to become adjusted to the situation before asking him to concentrate on his lessons.

OTHER DOGS IN THE AREA
Discourage your friends from bringing their pet dogs to watch yours practice. If someone does bring a dog, be sure to

ask him to either keep his dog in his car or on a leash well away from yours. If a loose, ownerless dog arrives on the scene, shoo him away and scold your dog if he has made a commotion. Sometimes the loose dog will not go away and will have to be tied. Sled dogs must learn to accept the presence of strange dogs in a dignified fashion, but loose dogs excite them more than tied ones do, and right now your dog has a difficult enough situation with which to cope without adding any extra distractions.

CONTROLLED RUNNING ON FOOT WITH ONE DOG

If you are starting with a dog that you can control on a leash and with whom you can keep up when he is trotting, it is best to give him his first few lessons with you on foot.

If you have your harness, put it on the dog for association. If you do not have it yet, you can start with just a strong collar and a line. Fasten the line to his collar and trot alongside him. If he goes a little in front of you, so much the better. As you are able, drop back behind him. You want him to go at a steady pace without stopping. If he does stop to sniff or lift a leg, say 'No!' and urge him on. You must be gentle but firm. He must also learn to ignore any loose dog that is in the area.

Whenever he starts out, give your 'Go' command in a high and happy voice. Say 'Whoa' when you want him to stop in a low-pitched voice and draw the word out. Give him a word of encouragement now and then but not a steady stream of talking. Give him petting and praise if you stop for a breather during your run, but save your most enthusiastic petting until you are finished.

The outing must not be play for the dog but must be enough fun so that he looks forward to the next time.

If you have a harness, put one lead on the collar and another on the back of the harness. Start out as with a collar only, but when you are able to drop back behind the dog, decrease the tension on the collar line and put the pull on the harness line. Unsnap the collar line when it no longer seems necessary, but be prepared to put it on again quickly if the dog gets out of control and starts to wander off the trail or stops to investigate something.

PROBLEMS

Dog Won't Lead Out: If the dog does not wish to go out in front of you, fool him into it by doing your training at a time of day when he is feeling his livliest, and train him at a place where he is more interested in the trail than he is in you. In this case don't scold him if he stops to investigate.

Eager Dog: Some dogs are so strong and so eager that they require handling by two people. Put one person on the collar line and the other on the harness line to hold the dog back. This type of dog needs strong jerks on the collar and a sharp 'No!' to make any impression on his mind. He is not being disobedient because he doesn't know what is expected of him, so don't become angry with him. He still needs praise when he does well and when he finishes.

Timid Dog: Sometimes a dog is so timid and unsure that when he sees the harness and line come out he goes off and hides somewhere. Don't let your dog get away with this. Pull him gently but firmly from his hiding place while talking to him in an encouraging tone. Keep your motions slow and steady and keep your voice calm. Don't reprimand him. He would not understand, and the tone of your voice would only upset him more.

When you finally get the harness and line on, the dog may lie down on his stomach or back, or he may just stand there with his feet planted. If he is lying down, lift him gently to his feet and hold him there. Don't jerk the line but use a steady pull. Keep the line low and the pull horizontal so that the dog can keep his feet on the ground. Sometimes a little tidbit of food in front of his nose will do wonders to get him going. Be sure to give him the food when he does move. You will not be spoiling him because when he becomes more sure of himself the food can be eliminated.

You can also try running away from the dog, with or without holding the leash, while enticing him to follow you. If he doesn't move willingly, crouch down in front of him with your arms outstretched and again call him to come to you. Be sure to give him enthusiastic praise for any progress at all.

Hysterical Dog: This dog is afraid and may bite in self

defense. Realize that his biting is from fright and not aggressiveness. Wear heavy protection and keep your face away from his. Instead of biting, he may jump around in all directions and try to slip his collar. Treat him quietly and slowly but firmly. Make sure his collar can't slip off, and use a steady pull on the leash. Do your practicing away from outside noise and confusion until the dog is more sure of himself and settles down.

SPEED vs LOAD TRAINING

A big question among sled dog trainers is whether it is best to teach a new dog first to pull a load or first to go fast. Those who favor teaching load pulling first feel that speed will come easily when the heavy load is removed. They feel that the dog who has been taught to pull a heavy load will never give up when the going gets tough. On the other hand, those who favor teaching the dog first to go fast feel that teaching the dog to pull a heavy weight accustoms him to going much too slowly. They feel that the dog develops a better attitude toward the sport if he is allowed to run fast because he likes to run. And finally, they feel that a dog who knows he is supposed to go fast will not slow down any more than necessary when the going gets tough.

You may wish to try both methods at sometime to see which one you prefer. However, the one you try first may well depend not so much on theory as on the equipment and trail available and your own physical stamina.

LEASH AND LOAD METHOD OF TRAINING

This method stresses pulling first and speed afterwards. It is to be used after the dog has started to learn controlled running on foot.

When the dog has become steady with the leash on his collar and has started to go out in front, attach a load to the back of his harness with about a three foot line. The load should be light enough so that the dog does not get discouraged trying to pull it, but not so light that it bounces around and scares him. It must stop when he does and not come up and hit him in the hind legs.

With the load attached, continue trotting with your leash attached to the dog's collar. If he is reluctant to start out, you may try going a few yards away and calling him to you. Remember that any dog who is pulling must, by the mechanics of his build, keep his head low; so when you call him, crouch down so that he does not have to lift his head to see your face. When he is trotting well, fall back behind him a little way. Eventually you must snap the leash to the rear of his harness. As he goes faster, you can increase his load until it approximates pulling a person on a wheeled rig.

Things to remember: If the load sticks on anything, do not move it yourself if the dog can. Urge him to pull harder. You do not want to teach him that as soon as the going gets a little tough, he can stop and have someone help him.

When your dog is pulling a load at such a speed and for such a distance that you can no longer keep up with him, you must get a vehicle for yourself.

USING A VEHICLE
Use a vehicle when you can no longer keep up with the dog on foot; or use a vehicle right from the beginning when the dog has no psychological problems and when you want to teach speed before you teach pulling.

CHASSIS OR SLED
Two people known to the dog should be available, if possible, for the dog's first few outings. One must be on the vehicle to prevent its coming up from behind and hitting the dog in case of a sudden stop. The second person starts out controlling the dog with a leash attached to its collar.

The first time a dog is hooked to a chassis or sled, he may do just about anything. Whatever his antics are, they are undoubtedly due to his uncertainty about what is going to happen. Ignore them and go about the business of hooking up as quickly and quietly as possible. The sooner you get going the better.

When all is ready, unfasten the vehicle and give the command to 'Go'. The person on the leash should run with the dog a short distance, and if all goes well, he should unsnap the leash while both he and the dog are still running. Once a dog gets going in the right direction it is best not to stop him, since the dog may turn around and/or get in a tangle.

If the dog does not run well after being started for a short distance or the leash, alternate methods can be used. The person most known to the dog can run slightly ahead of him while calling to him to follow. If the dog is fast, the person may need a good head start, but he must make sure that the dog sees him go down the trail and knows where he is. Hopefully, when the dog catches him, he will pass him by and keep going.

If the trail is suitable, the person most known to the dog can drive a car well in front of the dog and call to him to follow. In extreme cases, the dog and vehicle can be led away from the holding area, turned around, and then the dog allowed and encouraged to run back. Most dogs will come in better than they will go out.

Once the dog is going, the person on the vehicle takes over giving all commands and corrects the dog. If it becomes hard for the dog to pull the weight, the driver must either pedal the vehicle or get off and run behind or alongside it. The dog must not have to work so hard that he becomes discouraged. If there is any choice, the dog should not be trained on a rough or uphill trail that will slow him down.

AUTOMOBILE

An automobile can be used in the beginning when no sled or chassis is available.

Teach the dog controlled running by having him trot beside the car with the leash attached to his collar. One person should work both dog and car, holding the dog with one hand and driving the car with the other, so that the car can be made to respond immediately to the dog's actions. The length of line on the dog depends on the width of the road. The dog should be running abreast of the driver. The dog must not be held in too close to the car, but neither should the leash be so long that he loses the feeling of control.

Start out going no faster than *5 m.p.h.* Give all commands even though the leash is guiding the dog. If the dog seems afraid in any way, give him verbal encouragement and slow down. Often the speedometer will not register at all. If the dog stops to sniff or lift a leg, give him a sharp 'No!' and keep going, but be careful not to jerk him. If he wishes to run instead of trot, by all means encourage him to do so, as long as he is not darting all over. Always remember that it is not safe to go over about *7 m.p.h.* with an untrained dog so close to the car.

As the dog gains confidence, adjust the length of your line so that he is consistently running ahead of you. You must not let him get in front of the wheels, but you want to wean him away from always being right next to you.

When you get the harness, put it on him so that he associates running with the harness, but at first leave the line attached to his collar. When you are sure the dog is running confidently in front of you, move the line to the back of his harness.

If you are training two dogs, when they are both running confidently, put them together. Fasten the collars with a double neckline. Use a double lead line so that one line in your hand controls both dogs.

When your dog gets to the stage that he is really eager to go and can be depended upon to run steadily about a mile with his line tight all the time, then he is ready to be attached to the front bumper. The arrangement of ropes used to hook the dog to the bumper will depend on the individual car. The important point is that all ropes be strong and well tied and that about 20 feet of line separate the car from the dog. If the dog stops suddenly or turns around to come back, there must be enough room to stop the car before dog and car meet.

If you have a helper, have this person run alongside the dog at first to make sure he goes out steadily. Don't stop the dog once he gets going. If the helper has another car, he can follow you in case you need assistance.

After you start, adjust the speed of the car to the dog to keep an even amount of tension on the line. The dog should not be held back, but if the line becomes slack, there is danger of its getting caught under the wheels. After a few runs when the dog is going steadily, slow the car down just enough so that some load is put on the line and the dog has to pull a little. In his eagerness to go, the dog will learn to pull without noticing it.

Don't put so much load on the dog that you slow him down appreciably. However, if he wants to go over about 10 m.p.h. you had best get a sled or chassis quickly because it is not safe to go faster than that with a dog attached to a car.

BICYCLE

Using a bicycle is recommended only when no chassis or sled is available and the dog is already partially leash broken. The advantages of using a bicycle are: Most people have one readily available; it has a steering mechanism. The disadvantages are: The trainer has little control; the brakes of a bicycle will not hold a strong dog; getting on and off to correct the dog is more difficult than with a chassis, and if the dog suddenly decides to dart sideways, the driver can take a nasty spill. Although training with a bicycle has been successful for some people, it can be hazardous for others.

A harness and two lines are necessary. Fasten one line between the harness and the bicycle. The other line is snapped to the dog's collar. In the beginning, as the dog pulls one person on the bicycle, another runs alongside the dog controlling him with the line attached to his collar. As the dog becomes steady, the line can be removed from the collar.

When only one person is working the dog, the line from the harness is not attached to the bicycle. It is laid across the middle of the handle bar and held with one hand. It should run THROUGH the hand and NOT AROUND it. Care must be taken that the loose end does not get caught in the wheel. In the event of trouble, let the line run through the hand to avoid a violent jerk.

TRAINING SEVERAL DOGS

If all the dogs being trained are beginners, train them separately at first to minimize tangles and confusion. Start putting them together as soon as they seem to start to know what is happening. Put only two or three dogs together at first. The advantages of putting them together are that they give each other confidence and they can share the pulling load. In the beginning, put together only dogs that know each other well.

If two people with one or two dogs each wish to get together to make up a team, they should do so since such an arrangement can work quite well. The dogs get to know each other and will be kept at the same level of training. It is much easier for two people to train new dogs than one person alone. particularly when the dogs get to the stage of being hooked up together. It is also nice to have sociability and the chance to discuss problems with someone.

POSITION TO HOOK DOGS

If you have only two dogs and they know each other and get along well, put them in double lead. If they bother each other or play too much together or one does not seem to like the front position, put one behind the other.

If you have three or more dogs, consider each one's attitude and sex. Put dogs of opposite sex together if possible. If there is any question of one dog's not liking another, put him separately. The only disadvantage of putting a dog separately is that he is more apt to step over the towline than if there is a dog opposite him helping to hold it up.

If you have one dog that is so timid that he won't go out, have a handler walk him to the end of the trail and hook the dog in the team for the return trip home.

Try your dogs in different positions to see where they do best. Some like the right side, some like the left, and others do not care.

As a general rule, put the eager dogs at the front of the team and the timid ones behind. Some dogs like to be up front and some are not psychologically suited for that position. Often dogs will change from day to day. One day a dog will do well up front, and the next day he won't go out at all. It is not uncommon for an experienced driver with a well trained team to observe the attitude of his dogs in the starting chute of a race and at the last minute move his leader back and put up another dog. Likewise, it is not uncommon for drivers to switch leaders out on the trail. Always be alert to your dogs' moods and adjust their positions accordingly. If you can, try to figure out what conditions make the dogs' moods change.

TANGLES

All dogs get into tangles at one time or another with lines, harnesses, other dogs, bushes, or anything else that is within reach. To avoid tangles, first make sure that you never start out unless all lines are straight. If someone is helping you, have him hold the lead dog by his tugline. The handler is not to stand in front of the dog so as to block his view of the trail that he is to take. Neither is he to keep the dog immobile and quiet. He is to hold the towline between the dog and the vehicle tight to minimize tangles. If a tangle occurs in any dog's line, he is to straighten it out just before the team takes off. If it is convenient and no strain on the dogs, take the handler with you on the run so that he can help when necessary.

When a tangle occurs on the trail, analyze it to see if it will hurt the dog. If it will not, leave it alone and let the dog learn to get out of it by himself. A dog can easily get a leg back on the proper side of the towline. A little pressure taken off the line by increasing the speed of the vehicle sometimes makes it easier for the dog to free himself. If the tangle is going to hurt the dog or is of such a nature that he cannot possibly get out of it by himself, such as when a towline gets completely wrapped around a hind leg, then you must stop and straighten it out yourself.

The day will come when you will actually have to take a harness completely off a dog to straighten a tangle. Once in a while a tangle of such intensity occurs that a dog must be cut loose. The experienced driver usually carries a knife in case of such an emergency.

Novice dogs can get themselves into the most awful messes, so be warned. But also take heart; the seasoned sled dog almost never lets anything go wrong.

DISCIPLINE

Do not discourage your dog from getting excited during hitching up time. Discipline at this crucial point for showing his joy of running will only confuse and discourage him. He will be harder for you to cope with when he is jumping around, but he will run better for not having his enthusiasm squelched.

Common misdemeanors that do require some degree of reprimand are:

    a.   Turning around and coming back to you.
    b.   Taking the wrong trail.
    c.   Being generally lazy.
    d.   Fraternizing with loose dogs or those on another team.
    e.   Following small game off the trail.
    f.   Stopping to lift a leg.

If you have given the dog plenty of time to relieve himself before the run, he should not have to do this. On the other hand, some dogs absolutely must b.m. on the trail no matter how much time you have given them before the run. It is something about the running. This is not cause for reprimand. Instead, just encourage the dog to keep running while he is performing. If a lead dog stops to perform, you have no choice except to stop and wait until he is finished.

    g. Picking a fight. Self defense is legal, as is a female's snapping at a male who is paying her unwanted attention.

Suit the degree of your reprimand to the seriousness of the offense. Never become angry, although sometimes you may wish your dog to think that you are. An Alaskan college professor once said, "A musher is the only person alive who can swear all day at his dogs and never lose his temper."

Never hit a dog. Discipline is by voice only. Even a fight can usually be stopped before it begins if the driver is alert and gives a good shout just as one dog is thinking about jumping another.

Remember that any reprimand must come as close as possible to the very moment of misbehavior so that the dog can associate the reprimand with his act or thought. Do your reprimanding out on the trail, not when you come back from a run. No matter what has happened on the trail, when you come back the dogs must be petted and made to feel happy about the run so that they look forward to the next time.

A WORD ABOUT WHIPS

Whips are for signalling only. They have no place on the beginning team because the driver can easily signal his dogs by voice or by use of a jingler (bottle caps strung on a wire). Too often the beginner thinks he must use a whip to train his dogs "the way the big drivers do" and ends up doing much more harm than good. A little knowledge is a dangerous thing.

Harris Dunlap, who is one of today's best drivers and trainers, does not use a whip at all. In driving dogs trained by others, he finds that those who have not had a whip used on them do better than those who have. He says that there are "physiological reasons for a dog to run better if he gives a conditioned response rather than an adrenalin-pumping fear response." (Harris Dunlap, personal communication.) "Scotty" Allan, the legendary driver of yesterday, says in his book, ". . .I don't use a whip on my teams. I carry a whip, just as a policeman carries a club, as a badge of authority. If a fight starts or a strange dog comes up and wants to fight, a whip is handy to head off further trouble. It is much more effective if the dogs are not used to it." (Allan, *op. cit.,* p. 300.)

BREAKING IN A NEW DOG WITH A TRAINED TEAM

Many people decide they would like to try their dog as a sled dog because they have a friend who has a trained team. They would like to have their friend hook up their green dog with his trained team. This is likely to be disastrous. The dogs of the trained team all know each other. The strange dog in their midst is at an immediate disadvantage. The new dog does not like being confined so closely to all those strange dogs and is wondering which one is going to jump him first, though probably none will do so. He is confused by all the lines and harnesses and the jumping and yelping. Chances are that he will either lie down, start a fight in self defense, or hold back so much that he is dragged. At best he will certainly not be at the same stage of development as the trained team and could not keep up with them for long. In short, he could be mentally ruined before he even starts.

The conditions necessary to have an untrained dog run successfully in a trained team are first that the dog himself be neither nervous nor aggressive. It helps if the trained team is all of the opposite sex. The trained team must be small and have a reliable leader. The new dog should be hooked up at the back of the team either with a trained dog of the opposite sex or alone. The team must go slowly and not very far. An experienced musher might arrange such a situation to accommodate a friend, but to ask him to do this more than once is an imposition, no matter how polite he may seem.

The tried and true way for an experienced musher to break in a new dog of his own is indeed to hook it up with a few of his trained dogs. Usually he does not have the time to train each new dog separately on lead, and if all conditions are right, it is not necessary to do so. If you ever add another dog to your little team, you may give him some leash training first if you wish; but if you are careful, you may also put him directly into your team.

If the new dog is an adult, give him enough time in the dog yard for the established dogs to accept him as one of the group before ever hooking him up. Use a small team with a reliable leader who will hold the line tight and prevent unnecessary tangles. Hook the new dog up either by himself or with one of the opposite sex. Start him out in wheel position close to the sled or chassis so that the established dogs do not feel that he is robbing them of their position at the front of the team. It may be necessary to lengthen the towline so that the noise of the sled or chassis does not bother him. Go slowly the first few times so he doesn't get scared, and only gradually allow the team to pick up speed. Do not go far.

If the new dog is a puppy that you have had for awhile, the older dogs will have become used to him. Take him to your training sessions so that he can watch. While he is still small, let him run loose with the team a few times if possible. Chances are that he will run alongside or behind the team. When you finally hook him in the team, make sure the leader is reliable and there are no tangles. Also be sure to go slowly the first four or five times. A dog who has had a bad experience on his first few runs may never get over it.

RESPONDING TO COMMANDS

Give all commands in the manner described in the **COMMANDS** section. Give them whenever the dogs do that specific action, whether they need the command to do it or not. For example, say 'Gee!' when the trail turns sharply to the right. Just hearing the command at the time of the action will help the dog associate the two and learn the meaning of the word.

The 'Go' command is easy to learn because the vehicle is released at the same time that the command is given. When the 'Stop' command is given, the brake is applied to the vehicle to reinforce the command.

The 'Turn' commands are given to the leader. Give them as described in the **TRAINING A COMMAND LEADER** section. Make all corrections as described in that section. It is not necessary to give the leader special leader training before putting him in front of a small team because a beginning leader of a beginning team can learn his commands right along with everything else. Just do not expect too much of him. The main thing is that if he is given a command to go a certain direction, he must go in that direction even if you must lead him there.

The 'Speed-up' commands are the hardest to learn because the ways to reinforce them are the least definite. Before giving the team a command to speed up, make sure the team is capable of speeding up. The dogs must not be too tired and the trail must be good. It helps to give the command when the trail starts to go downhill. When you give your command to speed up, make sure the team does speed up. You can use your jingler at this time so that the dogs associate the noise of the jingler with speeding up. Pump the sled or chassis to take the strain off the team. If necessary, get off and run. If the team still doesn't speed up, stop and rest it and then try again. If just one dog is slowing down or refuses to speed up, call his name in an annoyed tone of voice just before giving the 'Go' command so that all dogs will know that the command is for him only.

POINTS TO REMEMBER
1. Give all commands during the run so that the dog can start to learn them. Be careful how you give them.
2. Don't talk to the dog continuously.
3. Don't go too far the first few runs. In the beginning the frequency of the runs is more important than the distance.
4. The distance will be controlled by the condition of the trail, the weather, and the dog himself. Although you must not overdo the distance, keep in mind that a dog with his tongue hanging out is not necessarily any more tired than a person who has just finished one set of tennis.
5. Give the dog enthusiastic praise when he returns from a run.
6. Don't repeat a run on the same day unless there is a long time between runs and the dog seems enthusiastic to go.
7. Anytime the dog retrogresses in his accomplishments, do not hesitate to go back in the training to a place where he feels comfortable. His forward learning progress the second time around will be quicker than the first.
8. Although repetition is necessary to teach a dog, don't get in a rut. If a dog continually makes the same mistake and gets scolded for it, this is a negative situation. The dog probably makes the mistake because he does not understand. Try to find some way to change what *you* are doing so that the dog does the right thing and does not have to be scolded. This is positive training. It is a matter of understanding your dog and trying to help him.
9. Forget about the old time "macho" use of whips. Do not use one at all, even for signalling. As of October, 1990, ISDRA Race Rules give race organizations the option of prohibiting the use of whips for signalling. More and more race organizations are exercising this option. Whips are completely forbidden in Europe.

CONDITIONING

When all the dogs you are going to run have been put together as a team, then you must condition them to run for longer and longer distances. After the team can lope easily for 1/4 or 1/2 mile, then run them for a mile. When they can do a mile easily, try 1-1/2 miles. They should lope the whole time. Try never to put them in a situation where the trail is so bad or so long or the weather so hot that they just trot.

In the beginning, if the dogs slow down too much at a new distance, stop them to give them a rest. Sometimes you can go up and pet them. Stopping does not hurt the training program as much as letting the dog go on and on only trotting. A trotting team will never do well in a speed race. Of course if you are training for camping or some similar type activity, it doesn't matter whether the dogs trot or not. The teams of the long distance Iditarod race usually trot all the way from Anchorage to Nome.

If you plan to enter a three-dog class race, which usually goes three miles, try to have your dogs run that distance a few times before you enter; but do not run one distance exclusively or your dogs will learn to pace themselves for that distance only. Keep building your dogs up to longer and longer distances until the season is almost over. You will be pleased and surprised at how much progress they can make during a single winter.

After the summer lay-off when training resumes in the fall, start the team out on the same short trail that it began on a year ago. The dogs will probably lope the distance easily. Increase the length of the trail after only a few runs and keep increasing it quickly until you find a distance that seems to give the dogs a little trouble. This should be the starting point for your serious conditioning.

Each succeeding year as you start your fall training, you will find that the same team can start at a longer and longer distance. If you keep the same dogs, the days of the 1/4 or 1/2 mile trail will be long behind you.

DRAG SLED TRAINING

Drag sleds are similar to standard wooden sleds, but are made of steel and can be used on either dirt or snow. They are particularly useful on rough trails where there is little control of small, wheeled carts, or where the terrain is too dangerous for a heavier chassis.

The average drag sled weighs between 80 and 110 pounds and is only 3-1/2 feet from brush bow to the rear of the runners. The frame can be made of water pipe or thinwall tubing. Water pipe is recommended because it is easy to work with and can be welded, whereas thinwall tubing cannot. The only wooden parts are the runners, which are about three inches wide and one inch thick. The runner shoes are 1/4 in. steel bolted on. The brake is similar to that of a wooden sled's; however, it is made of steel and should be angled outward toward the rear so that it will slip up over rocks. (Mel Fishback, *"Drag Sled Training," INFO.* Winter 1974, pp. 9-11.)

Because of its construction, a drag sled cannot be easily damaged like a wooden sled. Therefore, it is particularly useful early in the season in areas where there may be too much snow and mud for wheeled rigs, but too many bare spots for standard sleds. Regardless of trail conditions, Mel Fishback says, "The drag sled will go over it all, though a good wooden sled might get broken up." (Fishback, *loc. cit.*) And unlike a heavy chassis, a drag sled has the advantage that "you can always get it out of a bad spot or through a narrow one." (Fishback, *loc. cit.*) Because of its weight and heavy brake which bites the snow or dirt better than a standard sled brake, a drag sled is easier to control than a cart or sled when it is pulled by a large team.

The philosophy behind training with a drag sled is that the team must work harder to pull it than a sled or cart; thus, it is used as a muscle conditioner early in the season. Also, as it requires more effort to pull, it is easy to detect which dogs are really working and which are not.

If you wish to train with a drag sled, begin with a small team and run only a mile or two. Then gradually build up to the size team and mileage you want. When training on roads with leaves or pine needles, the sled is almost as fast as when on snow. The dogs have sure footing and solid ground and can go quite a bit faster and further than on dirt. So take this into consideration when deciding how many dogs to hook up and how far to run.

A drag sled can be helpful in training young or new dogs as it doesn't make as much noise as a cart and is less likely to scare them. Nor will the speed be so fast that it will scare them.

DRAG SLED
Dave Walling shown with his metal drag sled. Dogs in background are being exercised on a mechanical walker. (Photos courtesy of Dave Walling)

PASSING

Sled dog teams must pass other teams efficiently and safely both during training runs and while racing. This takes practice right from the beginning, so take advantage of every training run pass to develop good habits. Passing during training and racing is much the same.

There are two types of passing: head-on and overtaking. Different techniques are used for each one.

HEAD—ON PASSING

When two teams spot each other on the trail, the dogs usually become more alert and pick up the pace. If the teams approach each other both using the middle of the trail, give your leader a 'Gee Over!' command. If all leaders learn to pass on the right side of the trail, there is less confusion. Passing on the right side is a custom, however, not a rule. If both teams are already on different sides of a wide trail, be it left or right, let them stay there. Be careful about using the 'Gee!' command if the pass occurs at a place where a trail leads off to the right which your leader   might take.

As the leaders come close together, give a 'Straight Ahead!' or 'On By!' command, just as you would if you wanted the leader to go across an intersection.

It is much better in head-on passing if both teams keep moving. If even one of the teams stops, that team is going to spread out over the trail and be a hazard. However, the trail may be so narrow or bumpy or crooked that slowing the team is necessary, and sometimes one driver must get off his sled to lift it out of the way.

PROBLEMS

1.   *One or more dogs cross over the towline of the other team.* This problem usually occurs when one team slows too much or stops.

Solution: Both drivers stop. If the dogs don't straighten themselves immediately, either one or both drivers must set their snow hooks, go forward, and pull the teams apart.

Sometimes this type of tangle becomes so bad that dogs must be unhooked. If this happens to your team, try not to unsnap both ends of a dog at once lest the dog wiggle free. A loose dog that cannot be caught will cause the team's disqualification in a race. While you may untangle dogs in the other team, do not unsnap them unless specifically requested to do so. To lose someone else's dog is even worse than losing your own.

As with all tangles, move with deliberate speed, but keep calm. Speak quietly to the other driver and keep repeating 'Whoa' or 'Stay' to your dogs. Watch for other teams arriving on the scene from either direction.

2.   *Your leader turns around to follow the other team.*

Solution: Stop the sled but do not set the snow hook. Jump off on the side to which the leader is turning. Run up and meet him head on. Grab his collar or harness, turn him in the proper direction, and run down the trail with him until he seems to be going smoothly. Hop on the sled as it comes along without going back towards it.

3.   *Your dog snaps at a dog in another team.* Your dog must be broken of this habit if it is to run on a trail with other dog teams.

Solution:

a)   During a training run, plan a slow pass with another team. Ask the other driver to plant a foot hard on the offending dog if he should snap, or

b)   If the dog snaps, immediately stop your team and run up to him. Scream 'No!' at him and shake him hard by the scruff of the neck, or

c)   Carry a passenger who can run behind the dog during a pass and if the dog snaps, surprise him with a hard slap on his rump.

d)   In all passes where correction is *not* planned, such as in a race, call the dog's name and give him a firm 'No!' just before the pass.

OVERTAKING PASSING

Under ISDRA rules, when a passing team comes to within 50 feet of another team, the team behind has the right to pass the team in front. To save both teams time and to comply with the rules, the driver in front helps the one behind pass. The sequence on such a pass is as follows:

1.   The passing driver picks the time of the overtake. He may wish to wait a little to rest his team if they have been chasing, or he may wait for a more suitable part of the trail. It is not wise to attempt a pass on a steep downhill or on a narrow trail that is twisting around trees.

2.   When the passing driver wishes to overtake, he calls 'Trail!' in a loud voice. When the passing driver gets the attention of the overtaken driver, he tells him if he wants him to slow down or to stop completely.

3.   The passing rule states that the overtaken driver must give way to the passing team whether he hears the call 'Trail!' or not. The intent of the rule is to prevent the overtaken driver from not giving way with the excuse that he didn't hear the call. Instead, it is the duty of every driver on the trail to be on the lookout for teams coming up behind him. Usually when a driver goes out, he knows which teams will be following him and which ones will be apt to catch him.

4.   When the overtaken driver hears 'Trail!' or when the passing team starts to overtake without having given a call, the overtaken driver slows down and guides his sled to the left side of the trail so that the leader of the passing team can go to the 'Gee' side as in head-on passing. It is a custom, not a rule, that leaders pass on the right side of the trail; if they do, it is less confusing for everyone.

5.   As the sled in front gives room, the passing driver urges his dogs forward. If the pass takes too long, or if the passing leader slows down to the speed of the overtaken team, or for any reason whatsoever, the passing driver may at any time re-

quest the overtaken driver who has only slowed down to stop completely.

6.   If the passing driver requests that the driver in front stop before the pass is attempted, the overtaken driver should stop just as the following lead dog comes up to the rear of his sled. If he stops too soon, his team will scatter across the trail. After he stops, he should lift his sled toward or even off the left side of the trail if necessary and possible. However, he is not obligated to do so if it might mean that his team will get away from him.

7.   The passing driver has the obligation to do everything possible to keep his sled from hitting the other team's dogs as it goes by. On a narrow trail he may have to get off and lift it while running with it.

8.   During the entire pass and for some distance afterwards, no shouting or other loud noises should be directed by either driver at his team. Although a team is used to the commands of its own driver, the noise of another driver may terrify it. Hitting any object against the sled should not be done. Any noise, vocal or otherwise can be called interference by the other driver and can be cause for disqualification.

9.   Tangles seldom occur between teams during an overtaking pass. But the passing team often gets in a tangle due to its dogs trying to avoid the overtaken team. Since the passing team is obviously the fastest, and since repeated passing loses time for both teams, if a tangle occurs in the passing team during the pass, its driver may ask the overtaken driver to wait - see rules for time allowance for each class - while he straightens out the tangle. He should signal the overtaken driver that he is going to stop, particularly if he has started up before noticing the tangle. However, he does not have the right to make the overtaken team wait while he changes positions of his dogs or straightens out tangles that occured before or after the pass.

10. When the passing team gets going, the overtaken team must follow at a distance of its own team's length. This means that the lead dog's nose is a team's length behind the rear end of the sled in front. To let the lead dog follow closer than this distance can interfere with the driver ahead and can be cause for disqualification.

11. The overtaken team must stay behind for certain time and mileage intervals in each class unless the passing driver signals the overtaken driver to repass sooner. If during the 'forbidden-to-pass' intervals the passing team stops for any reason other than to undo a tangle which occurred during the pass, the overtaken team may repass immediately.

12. Under ISDRA rules, a point on the trail is marked as the start of a no-right-of-way-zone. That point is usually 1/2 mile from the finish line. The trail between that point and the finish line usually widens. When this zone has been reached, all previously stated right-of-way rules are void and teams may pass as they are able. However, no interference with other teams is allowed.

PROBLEMS

1. The overtaken driver does not hear the 'Trail!' call or the request to stop, does not look around, does not slow down or stop, and your team has trouble passing. This can happen when it is windy or very cold and the driver is wearing heavy ear-muffs.

Solution: If the problem occurs during a training run, discuss it with the offending driver after the run. If it happens during a race, submit a formal protest to the Race Marshall/ Chief Judge. At the discretion of the Protest Committee, the offending driver can either be given a warning or can be disqualified.

2. The passing leader will not overtake. He stays behind the forward sled, sometimes even stopping when it stops.
Solution:

a) If your leader won't pass because he is tired (it's a long race or he has been chasing) drop back and give your dogs time to get their second wind before trying the pass again.

b) Wait for a wider part of the trail or a slight downhill, which will encourage your leader to pick up speed. Ask the overtaken team to go very slowly or to stop completely.

c)   Ask the forward driver, as a courtesy, to pull your leader around his sled and as far forward as he can reach.

d)   Run up yourself, and pull your leader past the entire team.

e)   Stay behind the forward team until the end of the race.

Although you could legally keep trying to pass until the no-right-of-way zone, sometimes staying behind will save you more time than passing.

3.   *The passing team crosses over the towline of the forward team.* This happens when the overtaken team is stopped and spread across the trail, usually to turn around to see who is coming.

Solution:

a)   Request the overtaken driver to go ahead slightly, as that may separate the teams.

b)   Run up to separate the teams yourself.

4.   *The passing team slows down considerably after the pass.* This situation is common.

Solution:

a)   The forward driver spurs his team by whistling or other "non-interfering" sounds and by pedaling or running.

b)   The forward driver may request or agree that the following team re-pass even though the legal time and mileage intervals have not been reached.

c)   The next time, the passing driver does not pressure his team to catch the forward one. He lets them come up slowly to conserve their strength. Then they will be more physically able to speed up after the pass than if they are completely winded by the chase.

5.   *The passing team has a tangle that takes more than the legal time allowed to fix.*

Solution:

a)   The waiting driver should inform the forward driver that his time is up and then proceed to pass him slowly.

b)   If the forward driver has a safety problem, it is only sportsmanlike for the waiting driver to either continue to wait or to offer to go up and help.

6.   *A third team comes upon two passing teams with either one or both in a tangle.*

Solution:

a)   If there is room for the third team to pass either on or off the trail, he has the right to pass both teams.

b)   If either of the teams is in an emergency situation, it is only sportsmanlike for the third driver to stop and either wait on his sled or offer to go up and help.

TRAINING YOUR LEADER TO PASS

The best training is to practice passing every chance you get. On training runs, make arrangements with other drivers to set up passing situations. Owners of large kennels often divide their dogs into two teams, and with a handler driving one of the teams, the two teams practice passing and re-passing each other.

If you can break in your new leader with an experienced one, by all means do so. Always start a new leader on the going-home part of the trail, as in his eagerness to get home, other worries he may have will be minimized. For the first try, put the new leader on the side away from the team he will be passing. When he does not seem afraid of the other teams, move him to the near side.

HEAD–ON PASSING

Arrange your first pass for a time when the team is going home. Your leader is less likely to stop or turn around. Slow your team down, but do not stop.

On any pass, going home or going out, if the leader stops or turns around, get off the vehicle fast with no setting of the brake. Run up and grab the leader's collar or harness and lead him down the trail. Catch the vehicle as it goes by. Always praise the dog for his pass.

OVERTAKING PASSING

Try your first overtaking pass on a training run. Arrange it for a time when your team is not tired. Request that the overtaken driver either slow way down or stop completely. Pedal or run with your vehicle so that there is as little drag as possible on the team.

If you are running a new leader in single lead and he balks at the pass, get off your vehicle, run up to him on the outside, and lead him past the stopped team and a short distance down the trail. After the leader is going ahead on his own, let him go and then catch your vehicle as it comes by. Give him praise for his good pass.

If after four or five tries your new leader will still not make the pass on his own, hook up your most eager dog with him. Sometimes just having another dog with him whether it is a leader or not, will give him confidence.

BEING PASSED

When it is your turn to be passed, practice all right-of-way customs. Help the passing team get by as quickly and as easily as possible.

POINTS TO REMEMBER

1. In a head-on pass, both teams keep moving.
2. Don't push a team to catch one in front.
3. A passing team has all the rights.
4. An overtaken team must slow down, give way, and stop if so asked.
5. Neither driver interferes with the other team by making loud noises before, during or after the pass.
6. The overtaken driver must wait a specific time while the passing driver fixes a tangle that occured during the pass.
7. The overtaken driver must follow at the correct distance for the correct time or mileage interval.
8. If a leader refuses to pass, lead him by the other team. Dr. Lombard had to do this with his well-trained leader, Diamond, when the dog suddenly refused to pass.

He hooked up two seven-dog teams, and he drove one and his wife drove the other. The teams passed and re-passed each other many times with "Doc" leading Diamond each time until the dog regained his confidence. This technique will also work with small teams of only three dogs.

9.   It is nice after a pass for the passing driver to call or wave "Thank you".

TEAMS PASSING
Randy Roe passing Len Miller during a Sisters, Oregon race. Leading Randy's team are Targhee hound Chiquita and Alaskan husky Bull. (Photo by "Mally" Hilands).

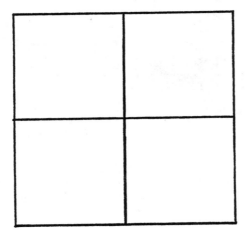

LEAD DOG TRAINING TRAILS
(Design and drafting by Daphne Rippon)

TRAINING A COMMAND LEADER

CHOOSING A DOG TO BE YOUR LEADER

If you have only one dog, of course he is the one you will train to be leader. If you have several, all of them should be tried in lead at one time or another to see what happens. To help you decide which one to try first, here are the points large-kennel owners take into consideration when they are deciding who to train for lead.

a) Eager to run.
b) Pays attention to owner.
c) Not afraid of other dogs.
d) Can take pressure (does not hide, dart off trail, or lie down on stomach).
e) Is not a fighter.
f) Can be reserved (many famous leaders are).
g) May or may not like other people.
h) Can be either male or female.

One common mistake that beginners make is that they have one favorite dog which they decide ahead of time is going to be their leader. No matter how badly the dog reacts to the training, they are blind and keep trying. Some dogs just do not like to run at the head of the team. Others don't like to run anywhere else.

LEADER TRAINING TRAILS

For special command leader training, you need a series of interconnecting trails where the dog has a definite choice of trails and must make a decision which way to go. Ys or Ts are best. Intersections are a little harder because the dog has three choices instead of two, but they are good for teaching the dog to go straight ahead.

If you don't already have a suitable trail, you can make one. If you have a field of high grass, you can mow your leader training course. If your field is snow-covered, you can pack it with a snowmobile, skis or snowshoes. If you have a cut lawn or dirt area, you can mark trails with stones, bricks, cut brush, or stakes with rope attached. You need only a visible track for the dog to follow; you are not trying to contain him.

If you start with one dog, make the course short enough so that you yourself can run around it several times. But it also must be long enough between turns so that the dog doesn't become confused by too many commands too close together.

Other types of command leader training trails are described in Raymond Thompson's *Cart and Sled Dog Training*. On page 20 he suggests putting a large obstacle in the middle of a wide trail, thereby forcing the dog to choose one side or the other.

On pages 39 and 40 of the same book, Mr. Thompson tells of the methods of Larry Folger of Alaska. Larry used snow shoes to put in a side loop on each side of his regular trapline trail. Sometimes he walked ahead of his single leader on a frozen lake or river which had two or three inches of fresh snow on it. He made many sharp turns, saying the turn commands as he made them. Then he let the dog lead him back and gave the commands just before the dog made the turns.

TRAINING ONE DOG ALONE
WITH THE OWNER ON FOOT

Put on the dog's harness so that he knows he is doing sled dog training. Use two collars with a leash attached to each one. (Obedience chains may be used instead of regular racing collars). Stand behind the dog, or alongside if necessary, and with one leash in each hand, hold the leashes out to both sides. Urge the dog to trot. If you must start out beside the dog, drop back as soon as possible so that he is running in front of you. As you come to a turn give the turn command as described in the **COMMANDS** section starting about 15 feet before the turn. If the dog does not go in the desired direction, stop, pull back and say 'No!' firmly. Repeat the turn command. If he looks back at you as if asking what you want, point in the direction you wish him to go and again repeat the turn command. If he still does not take the turn, guide him by the leash in the direction you want him to go with a series of short jerks. If you must, go down the trail yourself while *repeating the turn command* and jerking him to follow.

When the dog starts to understand the exercise, use only one leash attached to the back of the harness. Either hold the loose end or fasten it around your waist. When the dog wants to go the wrong way, guide him by the tugline rather than pull him by the collar. He will get the feeling that he is doing the action himself rather than being forced into it. Guiding seems to connect in his brain better than pulling. Of course he should always be praised when he takes the proper turn, even though you may have guided him into it.

Opinions differ as to whether you should teach 'Gee' first and then 'Haw' and finally mix the two together, or whether you should mix the two together right from the beginning. Perhaps this question will best be answered by your training trail. If teaching just one command at a time will only result in the dog's going around in a circle, teach both together. Otherwise, teach 'Gee' first, and start on 'Haw' when the dog has mastered 'Gee'.

You may go around your course several times, but for only about 10 minutes. The training must be fun for the dog and he must not become either tired or bored. After every training session, give the dog extra praise and a little play. The playing will make him look forward to the next session. And you must always keep in a good humor yourself, or at least put on a good show of it. If you are not happy, the dog will reflect your mood and will not do his best.

A dog trained to turn on command only should go straight through an intersection if he hears no command at all. However, most drivers believe a 'Straight Ahead' command is a worthwhile reinforcement.

After your dog is fairly steady at 'Gee' and 'Haw', you may

start to teach him 'Straight Ahead' or as it is sometimes called, 'On By'. Give your chosen command several times while he is going straight. Then finally give it before an intersection that he is to go through and continue giving it until he gets through. Eventually you will need to give only one command, but give it before the intersection at the time when the dog is making up his mind which way to go. Some drivers speed up when they are approaching an intersection where they want to go straight, as it is harder for the lead dog to turn sharply when he is going fast.

TRAINING WITH A VEHICLE
ONE DOG

A sled, a lightweight chassis or a bicycle can be used.

The advantages of using a vehicle as opposed to running on foot are that more distance can be covered so more turns can be made during the training session. Also, if trail conditions are good, the dog will be going at the normal speed he will be using on the trail. And he will learn to associate this training with pulling a load.

The disadvantages are that if trail conditions are bad, the owner will not only have to run, he may have to push the vehicle as well. Also, if the dog makes a mistake it will take the owner longer to get up to the dog to correct him.

Training one dog with a vehicle is basically the same as training him with a leash on foot. Give the same commands in the same way, although you may have to give them sooner before the turns if you are going faster. If you must leave the vehicle to correct the dog, don't anchor it. Run up to the dog, guide him to the proper trail, and lead him a short way down it with the vehicle following behind. Get the dog going, and then grab the vehicle and hop on as it comes along. At no time allow the vehicle to come up and hit the dog in the rear.

Bicycles are more readily available to the beginner than a chassis or sled. However, with a bumpy trail or a strong dog who is apt to dart off to the side, they can be dangerous. It is harder to get on and off them than a vehicle which stays upright, so it is harder to correct the dog when using a bicycle than when using a sled or chassis. For these reasons, use a bicycle only if no other vehicle is available and only with great caution.

A bicycle method of training is described in Frank and Nettie Hall's *Training Sled Dogs,* page 20. It involves attaching a pole to extend in front of the bicycle. A leash is attached between the dog's harness and the pole. Turning the bicycle after giving the dog the turn command pulls the dog toward the correct trail.

SEVERAL DOGS

As the leader becomes reliable, two or more dogs can be added behind him to give more pulling power and allow the team to go faster. Do not add dogs too soon because frequent stops are discouraging to the whole team.

It is more complicated to handle three dogs than one. There will be three dogs to stay stopped while you get up front. The wheel dogs are apt to get in a tangle while you are working with the leader. Then while you are untangling them, the leader is apt to return to the trail he wanted to take in the first place. When you finally get the team going, it is harder to catch the vehicle as it goes by because it will be going considerably faster.

If you are using a chassis and must anchor it to prevent chaos while working with the leader, either turn it over or only lock the brakes. It will still be somewhat movable so that you can drag it down the proper trail. If you are using a sled, set the snow hook lightly so that you can break it loose.

Anytime you must guide a leader to a different trail and leave him standing still while you return to your vehicle, return on the side that he came from. Once a leader has decided to take a certain trail, it is often hard to convince him to go somewhere else. The minute your back is turned, he will return to the trail he wanted to take in the first place. So keep an eye on him as you return to your vehicle. If he makes a wrong move, jump to block him, hold both arms out and shout 'No!'. Then maneuver him back to the proper trail and tell him 'Stay!' Sometimes it helps to point down the proper trail and tell him, "This is the way we are going to go!"

If you have two dogs that you are training separately to take commands, you can put them together in double lead after both have made considerable progress. This can work well, as long as one doesn't confuse the other. The two dogs usually give each other confidence, and you will have more pulling power.

When you put your whole team together and go out on a regular trail, handle your leader the same way you did on your training course. Use the same commands, the same timing, the same corrections, and the same praise. Just don't expect your leader to react as well as on unfamiliar trail as he did on a familiar one.

Even Dr. Lombard from Massachusetts had trouble with his well trained leader on the unfamiliar Anchorage Rendezvous racecourse. Doris Lake tells the story in the *1970 Fur Rendezvous & Dog Musher's Annual.* In 1958, "Chuckie tried every Avenue between 4 and 15. (I think that is where Doc's hair started turning grey) and he had to be led across every road crossing." The first two days in 1959 Chuckie did the same thing.

"That night he [Doc] sat figuring out a way that might help him, and finally went out to the shed for his towline. He decided to cut his team down to 7 dogs for the third day, and he rigged up what can only be called a jerkline. It was snapped to the ring on the lead dog's harness, taped at intervals down the towline, and tied to the handle bar of the sled. That last day he got as far as 6th Avenue when Chuckie decided to take the right turn. Doc stepped off his sled to the left, gave a hard jerk on the line to loosen all the tape and brought Chuckie to an abrupt halt with the rest of the dogs piled on top of him. Doc straightened the dogs out and started down Cordova again, but Chuckie had to try it one more time. When the same thing happened again the dog decided he had come out second best on that deal and got down to the business of traveling but was unable to get any higher than 9th place in total time. In the 'after-race' talk I commented that I would have liked to have seen the dogs when that jerkline snapped the first time. But Doc said with a chuckle, 'Dogs? I would have given anything to have had a camera to get the expression on the faces of the people standing there, when I stepped off that sled and just had a rope in my hand'."

TRAIL LEADERS

A trail leader is a dog that will stay in front of the team on a simple trail which contains no turn-offs. The Fairbanks, Alaska trail is this kind of trail as it is usually set in deep snow and has high banks. Thus, trail leaders are often called "Fairbanks" leaders even though they have never been in Fairbanks.

Trail leaders follow the best defined trail that they can see or smell. They will also follow another team and sometimes a skier or snowmobile if it turns in front of them.

The trail leader is apt to be the fastest dog on your team. Since he doesn't know commands, putting him in double lead with a slower command leader works well, as long as the command leader has the strength and desire to pull him on to the proper trail.

Putting commands on a trail leader is always good. The short trail, one-dog method might confuse a dog that is already used to going fast on a long trail, so save your training for times when you are on a regular training run with several dogs.

TRAINING LEAD DOGS WITH A HANDLER

If you have someone to help you, station him at a junction in the trail. Signal to him well ahead of time which way you wish to turn. In very beginning training, he can go down that trail a short distance and encourage the dog to come to him. Dogs will go toward a member of the family more readily than towards a stranger. The handler should stand well off the trail as the team goes by.

In later training the dog must learn to take the turn without outside encouragement. The handler stays at the junction and if the leader does not take the proper turn, the handler either leads the dog down the proper trail or grabs the vehicle to keep it under control while the driver maneuvers the dog. He keeps it from coming up and hitting the dog and he also slows it down when the dog starts to run down the proper trail so that the driver can more easily grab it.

Having trail help hold the vehicle and ride it with the brake partially on while the driver maneuvers the team a short distance onto the proper trail is allowed during a race.

LEADER TRAINING
Robyn Murer's Naklik and Kashak did not take the turn command at Leland Meadows, California   John Powell holds the sled. (Photo by Ed Murer)

USING A TRAINED LEADER
TO TEACH THE BEGINNING DOG

Hooking an untrained dog in double lead with a 'Gee-Haw' trained leader is the quickest and easiest method of teaching commands to a potential leader. This is how large kennel owners teach their new leaders.

Many beginning drivers purchase an older, trained leader to teach their own dogs. Older dogs are not as expensive as young ones in their prime, and often the owner of a large kennel is more interested in getting a good home for a favorite leader than he is in getting a good price. An older leader with a few years of running left is a worthwhile investment for the serious beginner.

The method of teaching is simple. The command leader will take the turns with confidence and the untrained dog will follow him. Sometimes the trained leader forcefully pushes or pulls the untrained dog onto the proper trail. The trained leader will probably prefer to pull rather than push the untrained dog, so put your command leader on the side of the most turns. Say your commands and make your corrections as described elsewhere.

STOPPING THE TEAM

Most race drivers do not specifically train their teams to stop on command as they are more concerned with their team's learning to go forward. However, when they do stop they say 'Whoa' or perhaps 'Easy' at the same time as they sink the brake. The dogs learn to associate the command and the sound of the brake with slowing down and stopping.

STAYING STOPPED

If you have a freighting or trapline team that you must go off and leave by itself, it is more important that the dogs learn to stay put than if you have a pleasure or racing team that you will be right next to all the time. Of course any team is easier to handle if the dogs will stay put on command.

The command to keep the dogs in place is 'Stay!' Unlike the commands to go or turn, the name of the dog is not said first as hearing his name might start him moving. Just say the command quietly, but firmly.

To practice the exercise, put a leash on your leader. Hold him in place with the leash and stand right in front of him. Still holding him in place with the leash, put the palm of the other hand in front of his nose and say 'Stay!' Back off about one foot and take your hand away. If he starts to move, say 'No! Stay!' and put your free hand in front of his nose again. Little by little, decrease the tension on the leash and increase the distance you move from him. If at any time the dog moves from his position, put him back where he should be and repeat the command. Don't hold him in position too long at first and don't give him praise while he is in the stay position or he might move. Save the praise until afterwards. Repeat the exercise for a few minutes daily until the dog stays while you move around as if working with other dogs on the team.

If you don't wish to take the time to teach the dog in a formal way to stay, you can give the command firmly often enough around the house, in the kennel, or on the trail — and reinforce the command when possible with your palm in front of his nose — and it won't take him too long to learn what you mean.

When working with dogs that are stopped, always be quick, but be quiet and calm so as not to excite the dogs into moving.

KEEPING THE LINE TIGHT

Some drivers train their leaders to hold the towline tight when the sled or chassis is anchored at the other end. This is handy if the driver has no one to hold the leader when he hooks up in the holding area because it will help prevent tangles. And of course it is handy on the trail when a stop must be made.

Teaching a leader to hold the line is an extension of the Stay exercise. The dog must not only stay in one place but he must keep enough tension on the line so that other dogs behind him don't pull him out of position.

Never spend so much time on or attach so much importance to staying and keeping the line tight that you dampen your leader's enthusiasm to run. After all, running is what this sport is all about.

RIDING THE SLED

Handling a sled is more complicated than is apparent at first, and the ease with which experienced drivers manage this skill makes most beginners think there is nothing to it. Often only after the first downhill turn when the sled goes out of control does the beginner start to ask questions. This section will attempt to answer those questions before you ask them. It will tell you why the sled reacts as it does and how you control it.

The most important principle in riding a sled behind a dog team is under all circumstances you should *help* your team. This means keeping a smooth pull on the gangline, not a jerking one; it means using your energy to smooth out the bumps in the trail; it means using the sled to avoid tangles; and it means not turning over.

RIDING THE SLED

Betty Allen racing at North Lake Tahoe, California. Lead dog, Tumulo, is a purebred Targhee hound. Another Targhee and two Targhee-husky crosses make up the rest of the team. (Photo by FREE-LANCE, INC., courtesy of Betty Allen)

BALANCE

The sled alone is relatively stable since its center of gravity is quite low, somewhere below the basket. The combination of you and sled together has a center of gravity near your waist or hips. The combination of sled and rider, with its higher center of gravity, is much more likely to tip over than just the sled alone. Therefore, lowering your body weight to lower the combined center of gravity improves the balance. Several ways of lowering your body weight are: a) bend your knees; b) squat down; c) lean forward over the handle bar, holding onto the side rail near the basket.

Squatting has the serious disadvantage of allowing tangles to go undetected because the driver can't see the team well enough. This position should be used sparingly and never when the team is starting up or running at top speed. However, if sometime you think you are surely going to turn over, "dragging your butt in the snow" for a few seconds may keep you upright.

Running alongside or behind the sled, holding it by the handle bar, lowers the center of gravity of the sled back to its original position and dramatically reduces its tendency to tip over. This running is useful when going over rough or uneven ground to reduce the strain on the team. Expert drivers with fast teams have been known to run around sharp curves, as this reduces the strain of the turn on the wheel dogs. Naturally, if you stumble and fall while running, you have not helped the team at all!

Sled balance can also be affected by the stiffness of the sled, the body of the driver, and by the rigidity of the hand hold. If both the sled and driver can give — or flex — when bumps are hit, the force of the bump is absorbed by the sled and driver. If everything is stiff, then even a slight bump can unbalance a fast-traveling sled. Such bumps are instantly transmitted to the team through the lines. Keep your fingers, wrist and arm muscles flexible. Keep your knees slightly bent and flexible. Relax! Don't be a "white-knuckle" driver.

CENTERS OF GRAVITY

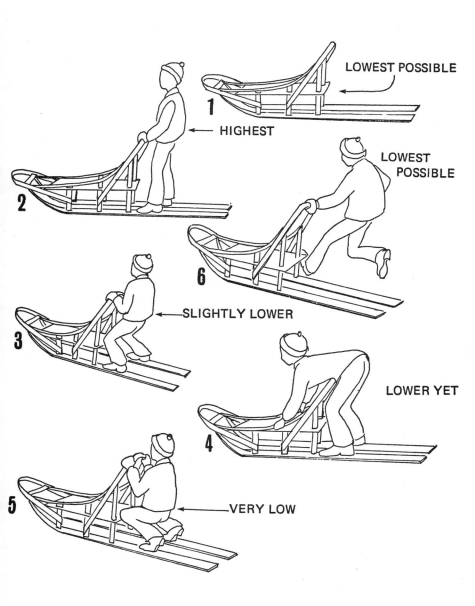

1 ← HIGHEST

LOWEST POSSIBLE

2

LOWEST POSSIBLE

6

3 ← SLIGHTLY LOWER

4 LOWER YET

5 ← VERY LOW

BRAKING

Using the sled brake to stop the team should be done with as smooth a backward pull on the line as possible. A slow, continuous, downward push on the brake is called for, with the command, 'Whoa', being given near the start of the braking process. This puts the least strain possible on the team.

Raising a foot off the runner and putting it on the brake, shifts the driver's center of gravity toward the side with the foot still on the runner. This should be counteracted by moving the upper body in the other direction. If the trail slopes to one side, keep your foot on the high side runner and let the low side foot work the brake. Being able to use either foot on the brake takes practice if you happen to be strongly right or left footed.

Braking can also be accomplished by dragging a foot. This is done by putting the heel into the snow just inside a runner. The ball of the foot rests on, or if your foot is small, against the side of the runner for stability. The ball of the foot should be pushed against the rear stanchion if great pressure on a firm trail is required.

Both heels can be used as brakes if necessary. But even with both heels digging in, there is usually not enough pressure to stop a well-moving team. Heel dragging is normally used when the driver wishes only to slow the team when approaching a section of rough trail, an intersection, on downhill stretches, or when going around corners. Toe dragging is not done as the toe can catch on hard snow or other trail imperfections, leading to broken bones.

Slight braking action can be accomplished by simply skimming the entire foot along the snow with light pressure. But don't let the toes catch.

Some sort of braking action is required whenever the gangling in front of you goes slack for any reason. Always watch for this and be prepared to act instantly. You may not want to lose even a second in a race, but braking until the line tightens will lose you a lot less time than letting it stay slack and getting a tangle.

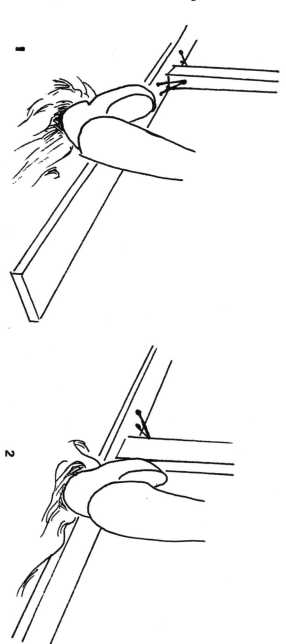

BRAKING

HILLS

Going down hills can be traumatic to the beginner because the sled wants to go faster than the team. Use heel dragging or as much pressure on the sled brake as is necessary to keep the gangline not just tight, but with a slight backward pull.

Why keep the gangline this tight? The reason is that dogs running free downhill can get going too fast. They can misstep and hurt themselves, particularly in the shoulders, or they can get so scared they won't ever run well downhill again. The backward pull on their tuglines keeps the dogs from running out of control and stabilizes them. If they feel secure, they will all run; if they are not secure, some will run and some will "put on the brakes" and be pulled. Just consider; would you prefer to run downhill at top speed without any support, or would you prefer to run just a little slower with a supporting backward pull on a harness?

If going downhill scares you as a driver, by all means slow down until you feel under control. It's far better to go slower for a short distance than to get yourself upset or run the risk of capsizing.

CHAINS

Working teams of the Arctic with heavily loaded sleds sometimes face hills which cannot be gone down safely with the sled brake alone. To increase friction, the driver stops at the top of the hill and wraps either rope or chain around his runners. He takes it off again at the bottom of the hill. Tuck this little fact in the back of your mind. You, too, may need it one day.

STEERING THE SLED

On a straight trail the pull by the dogs on the gangline keeps the sled on the trail. However, it helps if you can keep the sled tracking directly behind the team. On occasion you may wish to maneuver the sled to miss rocks, pine cones, bare patches, etc.

Weight shifting to one runner will steer the sled to a limited degree. The drag point of the sled tends to follow directly be-

STEERING THE SLED

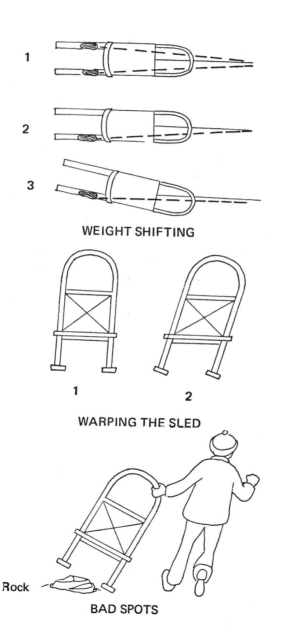

WEIGHT SHIFTING

WARPING THE SLED

BAD SPOTS

hind the team's center line. Thus, after changing the drag point from two runners to just one runner, the sled pivots, with the drag point moving to the center line and the brush bow turning in the direction of the weight shift. The sled then tracks slightly off course. However, it will not go far off course, unless the trail slopes down in this direction.

Dragging a heel has a similar, though more pronounced effect. It also slows the team down more than just shifting weight.

Warping the sled, or twisting it, will also steer it. This process involves physically bending the sled with the arms and legs so that each runner remains on the ground but becomes tilted. As the runner edges begin to bite into the snow, the sled starts turning in the direction of the low side of the runner.

Bad spots in the trail can also be avoided, or their effect on the team reduced by: a) lifting your weight off a runner about to hit a small object or small area of poorer trail b) running behind or, as experienced drivers prefer, alongside the sled through larger areas of poor trail surface c) tilting the sled onto one runner edge while running alongside to reduce drag on the sled and wear on the runners.

CURVES AND CORNERS

The most frequent cause of the sled's turning over, or capsizing is going around sharp turns. Centrifugal force causes the sled to slide toward the outside edge of the trail. As soon as the outside runner hits the edge of the trail, it stops sliding outward. If the driver himself is still moving outward, over he goes. If the driver counteracts the outward movement by leaning to the inside of the curve, his weight can prevent the sled's tipping over to the outside. However, if he overdoes it, an inside capsize can result.

Better than just leaning alone, is a combination of leaning and warping the sled to cause the sled runners to bite into the trail surface. This biting reduces or perhaps eliminates the sideways slide of the sled. Also, the warping and weight shift to the inside runner both act to turn the sled in the direction the team is going. As a result, the sled tracks right behind the team.

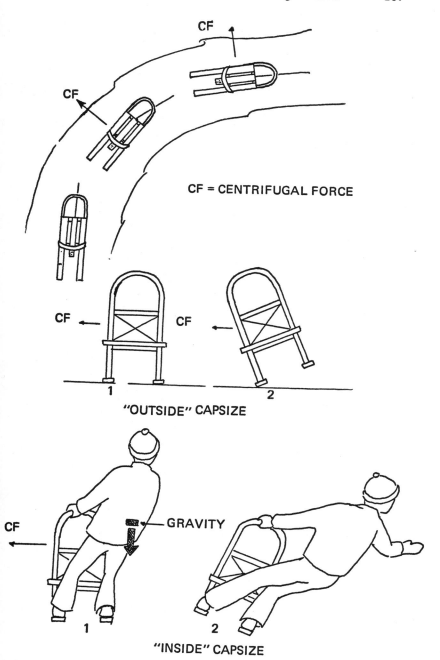

CF

CF

CF = CENTRIFUGAL FORCE

CF ←   CF ←

1   2

"OUTSIDE" CAPSIZE

CF ←   GRAVITY

1   2

"INSIDE" CAPSIZE

POOR SLED HANDLING: BRAKING AROUND SHARP CORNER

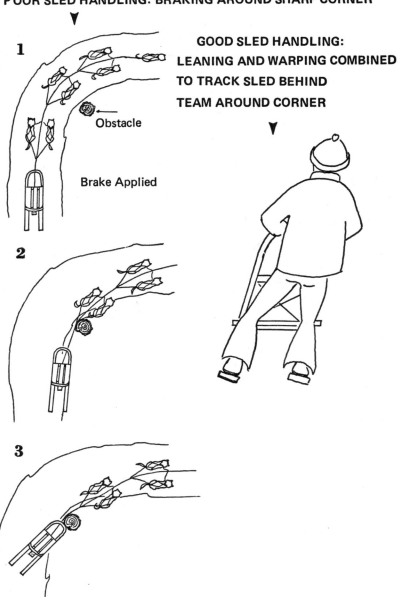

1

Obstacle

Brake Applied

GOOD SLED HANDLING: LEANING AND WARPING COMBINED TO TRACK SLED BEHIND TEAM AROUND CORNER

2

3

Braking and turning by dragging the inside runner heel is used on downhill curves, even if the curve is sharp, the team fast, or the trail slick. The driver usually crouches down or leans over the handle bar to lower the center of gravity as well. It must be noted that men with big feet can accomplish this heel braking and turning more effectively than anyone with little feet.

Braking by using the sled brake on curves and corners is not recommended. It tends to reduce the driver's stability, and on a sharp curve can actually pull the sled too close into the inside corner.

However, if you still want to use your sled brake at a sharp or fast corner such as on a downhill, use it *before* the corner to slow your team down, putting your foot back on the runner well before your wheel dogs reach the corner. Then lean inside and warp the sled only as much as required to have the sled follow the team and not slide to the outside. Don't overdo it.

If you still have too much trouble getting around corners, check how your bridle and gangline are fastened to the sled and the length of gangline between the sled and your wheel dogs. If there is too much play, the sled won't corner well.

Steering the sled with a passenger, human or canine, or with a heavy load, is more difficult than steering it when it is empty. If your passenger is a person, ask him to lean into the turns. Also ask him to take the bumps with his arms on a strong part of the sled so that he won't break the basket.

PEDALING

To pedal, or push the trail surface with one foot while keeping the other foot on its runner, is difficult to do effectively. This is because the forward push to the sled causes the tugline to go slack. The sled then decreases speed to slower than it was going before the pedal and, as the dogs pull, the tugline jerks taut before the next pedal can be started. This jerking is hard on the team, and many times the team is better off without your pedaling "help".

The solution is not to pedal faster with short leg strokes, as this only causes more frequent jerking. Instead, a long pedal stroke is used with a long follow-through. Movies of top drivers always show a good follow-through. As long as the foot is moving backwards, forward thrust is imparted to the sled. After the foot leaves the ground, the rate of the sled's acceleration decreases as the foot goes further back. Thus the sled slows down gradually as the dogs slowly take up the slack in the line. By the time the sled slows down to the dogs' speed, the slack is completely taken up. Result: no jerk.

BUMPS

Traversing bumps with no musher help results in a wide variation in sled drag, which jerks the dogs. On the other hand, pedaling is particularly difficult to do on a bumpy or rough trail. However, it can be effective if each pedal is individually placed just before each bump. The pedal drives the sled forward and reduces the uphill strain on the gangline.

Another way a driver can assist the sled and his team, through the bumps is by shifting his body weight. The process basically consists of quickly pushing the knees and body weight down and forward just as the sled starts up over the bump. The driver rises back to his normal position as the sled goes down the other side of the bump. Many drivers do this without realizing it. This process of shifting weight back and forth is widely used in sailboat racing to help a boat get through the waves. It is called "ooching".

UPHILLS

Your weight slows the team greatly on the uphills, so this is when you should be doing most of your running and pedaling. If the hill is long and you can't run all the way up, pick out the steeper parts for your running. However, don't tire yourself out so much that you slip and fall or have no strength left for tangles or other emergencies.

TURNING OVER

If you turn over, *hang on tight to the handle bar.* Usually a small team will stop and turn around to look to see what has happened. Sometimes the dogs almost laugh! But don't count

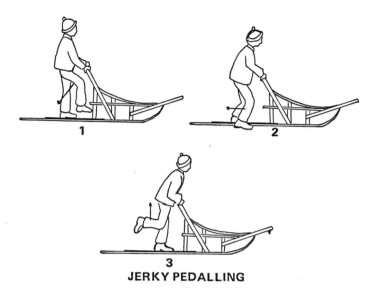

JERKY PEDALLING

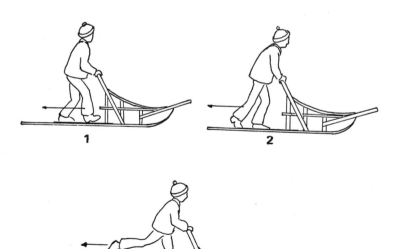

SMOOTH PEDALLING WITH FOLLOW THROUGH

on their staying stopped. Get both feet on the runners as quickly as possible.

If you are being dragged down the trail, try to right the sled and get one foot on one runner—or perhaps you can get only a knee on at first. If the sled is going fast, before it is righted, try to put a foot on the down runner. Then when you right the sled and the team goes even faster, you will already have contact with one runner. Pull yourself up and get the other foot on the other runner. Don't yell at your team to stop since yelling will only speed them up. A calm, low voiced 'Whoa' *might* help.

Sometimes, if snow conditions are right, an overturned sled and a dragging driver will stop a small team better than a brake. If a driver is desperate to stop and the brake is ineffective, he may turn the sled over on purpose and sink the snow hook while he is still down.

Native Alaskans have a saying: "Lose your team, lose your life," since losing a team many miles from camp at far below freezing temperatures can be fatal. Your biggest problem is not freezing to death, but that letting your team run loose down the trail can cause the dogs serious injury. Your wheel dogs and others can easily overrun dogs in front of them since you aren't there to make sure the line stays tight. Tangles almost always occur, and sometimes dogs fall and are dragged for long distances. So the cardinal rule is: "Don't lose your team! Hang on for their sake!"

Of course there may be times when you are being dragged and can see that you are going to be slammed into a tree or rock. If you are going to be forcibly parted from the sled anyhow, you will do better to let go and save yourself injury. Then you will be able to get up and run after the team.

PRACTICING RIDING THE SLED

You can actually practice riding the sled without a team. Try pedaling on a flat, smooth trail. Notice how follow-through helps. Ride down hills, particularly hills with curves. Get a tow from a snowmobile. Use at least a 10-foot hitching rope and watch out for sudden stops by the machine. This is a great way to get a preview of any trail.

As a beginning musher, you should also practice all aspects of riding the sled behind your team when you are having a good training run. Don't wait until you *must* use a maneuver. Try everything that has been mentioned so far until you feel at ease on the sled and gain confidence in your ability to control it. Then you will be better able to relax, and both you and the dogs will have more enjoyable runs.

EXPERIENCED DRIVER TIPS

1.   While small-team drivers can help their teams by running at the start, or after a trail stop, an experienced large-team driver rides the brake at the start. The leader may not have heard the command to go or may not be a fast starter. A tangle can happen very quickly. The race can be lost before the team has even gotten underway.

An actual case in point is the one of a not-too-experienced driver who came to the starting line of a major race with a long string of dogs. He didn't ride the brake out of the chute and a tangle soon developed. Before he could get up to the tangled dogs, he had a breeding—right in the middle of downtown Anchorage!

So large teams start with the brake partially on, giving the whole team a chance to get strung out and going smoothly.

2.   Crouching down reduces the effect of a head wind, but experienced drivers don't do it since then they can't see what their front-end dogs are doing. Instead, they lean over their handle bar and hold onto the side rail by the basket.

3.   To get around a very sharp corner, pedal just once as the wheel dogs make the turn. This shoots the sled straight ahead so that it doesn't cut the corner and hit a tree or bank. The sled will be spun abruptly around, so good sled control is necessary.

4.   Some Alaskans go around sharp corners like this: Move the outside runner foot backwards to the rear of the runner and push down hard. Warp the sled to put the runners in bite position. The drag by the rear corner of the outside runner helps swing the front of the sled around.

5.   Some drivers have been known to "jump-turn" their sleds like skiers. Jumping with the sled can also be used on a

straight trail to get the runners in a different rut; or if the trail has a side slope and the sled has worked its way down, it can be jumped back up behind the team.

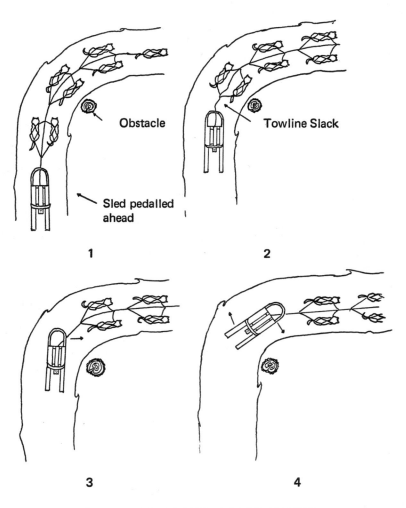

PEDALLING AROUND SHARP CORNER

BODY LANGUAGE

Dogs are honest. They don't know how to lie or deceive. Indeed, every movement they make is due to what they are thinking or feeling. While the position and the parts of the body taken separately all mean something, the attitude of the body as a whole must also be taken into consideration when interpreting what the dog is expressing. It is up to you to study your own dog and learn to interpret what he is telling you with his "body language".

HEAD

A head held high can show attention, curiosity, or dominance. A head held low shows confusion or submission. On the trail, a low head means the dog is pulling.

EYES

Eyes are the first line of communication. Watch them to learn which expressions means that the dog is uncertain, determined, enraged, frightened, fearful or distracted. Eyes that lack luster can mean that the dog is not feeling well.

EARS

Ears held high show alertness. One ear twitching to the side can indicate some distraction which may cause the dog's head to turn soon in that direction. Ears held high and wide can indicate uncertainty or curiosity.

Ears laid back and low while the dog is being stroked indicate contentment. Ears held low and back while training indicate attentiveness to the driver. If on the trail all ears suddenly stand erect, something ahead of you has caught the dogs' attention.

One ear hanging to the side, particularly if the dog is also shaking his head, probably means that something is in the ear.

MOUTH

Some dogs' lips curl into a 'smile' when they are happy or playful or when they are embarrassed. However, curling of the dog's lips when cornered or when pushed too far can mean trouble.

VOICE

Barking can mean boredom, play, feeding time or aggression. Some growls mean play; other growls mean trouble. Listen to your dog and learn what he is saying with each of his noises.

TAIL

A wagging tail indicates happiness, but that doesn't mean that if a dog is wagging his tail he won't bite you. Some dogs enjoy biting people and will wag their tails the whole time they are biting.

Learn the position in which your dog carries his tail naturally, and then be alert to changes in that position. Usually a tail carried low indicates placidness or rest. A high tail indicates attention and excitement. A tail slightly between the legs means uncertainty. A tail all the way between the legs or tucked up against the belly means extreme fright and confusion.

An erect and rigid tail, sometimes with slight movement, means trouble in the form of a possible fight.

If on the trail a dog who usually carries his tail straight back suddenly raises it, it means that he isn't applying himself and that he may start shortly to relieve himself.

HACKLES

Hackling is the raising of the hair over the withers, topline and croup of the dog. It indicates that trouble is brewing.

BODY

A dog who crawls or slumps low to the ground is lacking confidence. He simply does not understand. A dog who rolls over on his back may be showing confusion or he may just want his stomach scratched.

DOG FIGHTING

The writer of this chapter, Thom Ainsworth, has for many years been a licensed instructor at Guide Dogs for the Blind, Inc. in San Rafael, California. Prior to this, he was an Air Police Sentry Dog Handler in the United States Air Force. Almost daily he works with up to 38 dogs at a time loose in an exercise yard. He is also a sled dog driver.

What do you do to prevent your dogs from fighting? First learn what situations are apt to provoke a fight and take precautions to prevent those situations from occuring. Get to know each of your dogs' personalities and how each dog reacts to other dogs. Recognize when a fight is coming and stop it before it starts. An ounce of prevention is worth a pound of cure.

If the worst comes, you must break up the fight whether it is between just two dogs or your whole team. This chapter will tell you how.

SITUATIONS THAT ARE APT TO PROVOKE A FIGHT
BITCH IN SEASON

The odor of the bitch in season arouses the mature males and causes excitement and jealousy. Males in large kennels who are continually exposed to the odor do not seem to be as affected as males in a small kennel who smell it only once in awhile. Keep males separate from each other.

Bitches in season often do not like to be pestered by either dogs or other bitches. If the bitch in season snaps at a male, this is considered acceptable behavior and will not cause a fight because he won't snap back. But if one bitch snaps at another bitch, a glorious fight may follow.

PLAY

Play is fine; but when it gets too rough, a fight may develop. Any object such as a toy, ball or piece of wood may start out being something to play with and end up being something to fight over. Never throw a ball into a group of dogs.

WEAKER DOGS

Dogs have a tendency to gang up on a weaker dog. If he tries to get away from them, they give chase. When the weaker dog becomes cornered, he may snap and start a fight.

HURT DOG

Whenever a dog yelps from pain, or even fright, the other dogs are apt to jump him.

OLDER DOGS

As dogs get along in years, they become weaker. Old, dominant males are often challenged by young, aggressive males. If a fight starts, all the young males may gang up on the old leader.

NEW DOGS

New dogs are greeted with curiosity and suspicion. Introduce the new dog to your team slowly and carefully.

PECKING ORDER

Dogs housed loose together work out among themselves who is superior to whom. Sometimes, but not always, a fight is part of the process.

EXCITEMENT AND TENSION

Tension and excitement will build up when a strange dog appears either near the dog yard or on the trail, when any dog is loose and the others are tied, when teams gather at a training or race area, when a wild animal or cat is sighted, and many other times. When not calmed down, your own dogs may jump each other.

TERRITORY

Any dog that invades another's territory, whether on purpose or by mistake, may be attacked.

ADDITIONAL PRECAUTIONS
ON THE TRAIL

If two dogs on your team have had a recent fight, separate them as far as possible in the hook-up. At the first sign of interest in each other, call their names and tell them 'No!' Dog fights between teams are rare even when teams are tangled together during a pass.

GROUP RUNNING

An exercise yard 50' x 150' is large enough for ample exercise and yet small enough to maintain good control. Don't exercise too many loose dogs by yourself. Take care when letting the dogs out, as the most critical time is the first few minutes when the dogs are highly excited.

HOUSING

House together or next to each other only dogs that are compatible.

FEEDING

Keep all dogs chained or otherwise separated.

PERSONALITY

Dogs, like people, are individuals, each with their own personality. But this personality can change with age and with each situation. If a fight starts, be warned that a normally shy and docile dog can turn instantly into an aggressive maniac.

While dogs are apt to fight dogs and bitches to fight bitches, the two sexes will fight each other in a general free-for-all. Likewise, members of the same family are less likely to fight each other than they are to fight non-members, but don't count on it.

Knowing your dogs will enable you to anticipate and stop possible fights. As you work with your dogs, think about what they are doing and why they are doing it. Always be alert.

THE CHALLENGE

Sometimes male dogs will go through a preliminary routine indicating that a fight is about to take place. The two dogs will approach each other with rigid bodies and short, stiff steps. Stares are exchanged. Tails are held erect and almost motionless. Getting closer, the hackles begin to rise first about the shoulder and then along the top line. When the dogs are almost close enough to touch, they may circle slightly or stand cheek to cheek waiting for the first move. Though all these actions may take place in only a few seconds, they give you time to recognize the challenge and stop the fight before it gets started.

When bitches fight, their challenge sequence seems to be just a curled lip and a growl.

BREAKING UP A FIGHT

There are several ways to break up a fight, but in all of them it is important that you maintain complete control of yourself.

YELLING

Yell and scream as you run toward the skirmish. This extraordinary noise from you will often startle the dogs enough so that they forget the whole thing.

WATER

If you happen to have a water hose that is long enough to reach the dogs or a full bucket of water close at hand, a dousing will often be sufficient to stop the fight.

THROW CHAIN

A throw chain is about eight links of medium weight chain or a slip collar. The chain amounts to an extension of your arm and is often called an "equalizer". When you see a challenge, roughhousing, or other form of misbehavior, throw the chain at or near the problem. As the chain hits, give a loud 'No!' Dogs conditioned to a throw chain will soon respond to the jingle of the chain in your hand accompanied by your scolding tone of voice.

STICKS

Broom sticks, 3/4 in. plastic pipe, or any similar type implement slapped against a flat surface will often make a loud enough pop to stop a fight before it begins or to get the dogs' attention if the fight has not progressed too far. A stick can be used to strike fighting dogs across their muzzles with a short, sharp rap. Dogs respect a stick, and any stick just held in the hand of the owner is a great deterrent.

HANDS

If you have no implement except your hands, be careful where you grab, as even your own dogs will bite you. Go after the dog that is the aggressor or has the advantage. Yank his tail sharply and lift his hind quarters into the air as you pull him away from the fight. Scold and shake him. When all is quiet, lower him to his feet and separate him from the other dogs involved.

Grabbing and pulling the sensitive, loose flesh in the flank area can make one dog let loose of another.

Choking:

Should one dog lock on another with such a hold that you can't pry its jaws open, then it becomes necessary to choke the dog. Squeeze his windpipe by hand or by twisting his collar from behind his head. Be careful that you don't use so much force that you collapse his windpipe. You will know that enough force has been applied when you hear his labored breathing. As soon as the dog releases his hold, lift his front feet off the ground so that he can't get back into the fight.

BUNTING

You can use your feet either to break up a fight or to bunt other dogs away from one you have lifted up. Use your instep, not your toe.

GROUP FIGHTING

In a group fight, most of the dogs will go for the one on the bottom, although smaller fights may break out among dogs on the fringes. Usually one dog is the major aggressor while the others just want to get in on the action. Go for the worst aggressor first and get him separated or chained. Then go back to the fight and separate one aggressor after another until no dogs are left fighting.

FIGHTS ON THE TRAIL

If two dogs in a single team start fighting, pulling on one

dog's harness may free them. If it doesn't, apply the methods described above. Keep yelling 'No!' to the other dogs to keep them out of the fight. If two teams are fighting, both drivers must work together to break it up.

TEACHING A DOG NOT TO FIGHT

Some dogs are natural fighters. Try to socialize this type on a leash with a properly placed slip collar. Put the dog in a situation where he can show aggression but cannot reach another dog. When he goes for the other dog, jerk the leash sharply and give a harsh verbal correction. If the dog seems insensitive to the leash correction, slide the collar high up on the neck and just behind the ears to give the collar more bite. This type of dog may have to be jerked off his front feet and given a good shake while up in the air. Scold him at the same time. Then slowly let him down and walk him around the other dog. If he starts in again, repeat the correction. If this still doesn't work, try giving him a solid and sudden upward slap on the lower jaw while he is being jerked off his feet. Be sure to praise him for any good behavior.

If your dog cannot be broken of fighting, remove him from your team. It is not fair to your own team or to others to have a fighter in the holding area or on the trail. You can be disqualified if you have trouble. Even worse, you may have a lawsuit on your hands.

"SCOTTY" ALLAN'S DOG FIGHT

This fight is reported in Allan's book (op. cit. pp. 264–267).

In late 1915, "Scotty" Allan arrived in France from Nome with 440 Eskimo dogs which had been purchased by the French government to help in the war effort, and thereby set the stage for what has to be the biggest dog fight in history.

After training sessions with the 50 new French drivers (Chasseurs), Allan was in the habit of letting half the dogs loose at a time in an enclosure. He always stood in the middle of the enclosure watching for and ready to nip in the bud, any sign of trouble. Here is his version of what happened:

"One afternoon just before entraining for the front, I drove into town to purchase some extra snaps, chains and rope. I didn't get back as soon as expected. With good intentions, and never expecting any trouble, the boys turned the dogs out as usual. I was on my way back. When I got about a block from the abattoir I heard a terrible noise. I knew what that meant; a good, old-fashioned dog fight!. . .I told my driver to step on it. He did, after he understood what I wanted. Long before the car stopped I had hit the ground a-running.

I'll never forget the sight I saw on getting through the gate. There were about five or six piles of snarling, fighting mala- mutes having the time of their life; that is the ones on top were. Those on the bottom of the piles were getting smothered.

"The piles were higher than a man's head; in fact, so high that a dog would have to take a running jump to get on top of it! Once on top he would fasten his teeth in the one he landed on and start shaking and hauling him for all he was worth. When a dog broke loose from the one he was worrying he would roll to the ground, only to jump back on top of the pile or some other pile. . .It was a typical, Irish scrap such as I had seen at Stops Fair when I was a youngster. And such ear-splitting howls and snarls from every animal that had breath enough to yelp, I have never heard.

"No dog had it in for any one dog in particular. It was a case of whoever was nearest. And every dog was having a grand time! If they could have talked afterwards I am sure they would have said it was the greatest scrap of the whole war. I have seen hundreds of dog fights, and some big ones, but never one that was deuce high to this!

"The 50 Chasseurs were showing more action, if possible, than the dogs. . .Their hands, feet, and tongues were all work- ing hard, as each man was whaling away with a big whip at the various piles of dogs, every blow an urge to more bitter bat- tling. In fact, I suspect that the dogs thought they were taking part in the fight, rather than trying to stop it.

"The Chasseurs had completely lost control. The dogs knew it and were acting accordingly. They were amuck; indeed, if

it hadn't been that they were so intent on fighting amon
themselves they might have tackled the men. That sometim
happens with inexperienced drivers.

"I took in the situation at a glance. At once I made a deci
sion. If it worked it would be a good lesson to the boys in the
discipline and control of dogs. So far I had had a hard time
getting them to understand the necessity for handling dogs in
a humane way.

"If I could only make myself heard above the tumult I
thought I could quell the riot. I couldn't talk French but
there were a few of the boys who could understand some
English. I ran to them and begged them to get the rest of the
Chasseurs and go inside the building.

" 'When dog comes in, tie him up!' I shouted. I tired so hard
to make them understand that I began talking pidgin English.

"Moving the Frenchmen turned out to be harder than stopping the dogs. I thought we'd never get the excited soldiers to
quit pounding them. Finally I had to run in and drag some
away by main strength.

"At last when the Frenchmen were all inside the door of the
building I stepped to the center of the enclosure and during
the first lull gave the familiar 'Yeah Yon!' and popped my long
black, snake whip. The dogs heard and instantly recognized
my voice. Those on the edges scurried away.

"On the first crack the main scrimmage broke. Joy, I had
them! Quickly I followed up my advantage. For action during
the next few minutes I had even the Frenchmen faded! Only,
I wasn't laying my whip along the full length of the dog's
back. I'd pop it to them at long range when they flew for
their kennels. But every time the buckskin went out it brought
a yelp of pain that threw fear and dismay into the other vil-
lains with an effect that was amazing.

"The piles of struggling dogs melted like snow on a hot
stove. In a few minutes it was all over. Between 20 and 30
dogs were left lying on the field; but they all gradually came
to life except four, which I thought were dead. However,
some of the Chasseurs kept working on these and brought
them back to life.

"I felt we'd got out of the jam very luckily. Quite a few of the dogs had skin cuts or gashes, but nothing to incapacitate them from work. The ones I thought were dead didn't have a scratch on them! They had been smothered in the bottom of the piles."

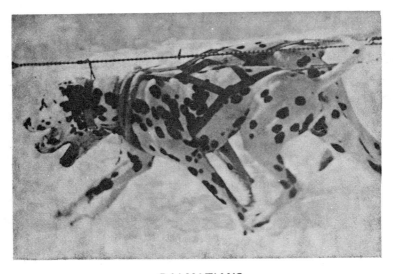

DALMATIANS
Obedience trained Baggins and Three Spot running on Gary Link's
all-Dalmatian team. (Photo by Nancy Link)

OBEDIENCE TRAINING and SLED DOGS

Many obedience trainers become attracted to the sport of running sled dogs because to do it successfully is a challenge to their ability. Also, after a length of time in obedience, they are ready to do something different with their dogs. They like the idea of vigorous outdoor exercise, and if they happen to have one of the northern breeds, they want to see if their dog can do what it was bred to do. But they usually don't want to give up their obedience role.

If you are one of these people and your dog has been working toward an obedience degree that you wish to finish, it is not necessary to abandon your efforts toward that end. Almost all obedience trainers maintain that the dog has enough intelligence to distinguish between a show lead, an obedience slip chain, and a tracking harness. There is even more contrast between these items and a racing harness. Many utility dogs take only once or twice in the tracking harness to become eager pullers after the trail. With the even greater motivation of keeping up with his teammates, the obedience trained dog quickly learns to lean into his harness with the best of them. The differences between sled dog training and basic obedience are so great that you can practice for one in the morning and the other in the afternoon without confusing the trained obedience dog. It is not suggested, however, that you *start* both at the same time.

SOME DIFFERENCES BETWEEN OBEDIENCE AND SLED DOG TRAINING

The most obvious difference between basic obedience and basic sled dog training is that the obedience dog is corrected if he pulls against the leash, whereas the sled dog is corrected if he doesn't pull. Correction in the latter is not a jerk towards the trainer but a verbal urging away from him.

Another difference is that there is no repetition of the same exercise on the same day, except for special lead dog training. The trainer must get his message across during only one trip around the course. Nor do teams in training go out every day all year long. A few times a week for only part of the year is standard procedure.

In sled dog training more attention is paid to the attitude of the dog. In beginning obedience the dog does his exercises because the trainer tells him to, and then, if necessary, the trainer reinforces his command with the leash. The sled dog runs for the sheer joy of running. The driver can't *make* the dog run; he can only control the dog's speed and direction.

Verbal communication is less frequent in sled dog training than in obedience. Talking is done only to give a command or a word of praise or encouragement. With the distance covered measured in miles of trail instead of feet in a ring, there will be long periods of silence. When the obedience trainer does speak on the trail, he should re-educate himself to speak more quietly than he does when he must be heard over the noise and confusion of the training class or obedience trial. In the silence of the trail, any dog can hear the slightest noise.

Obedience trainers always find that one of the more difficult aspects of training is to get the dog to work when it is not close to the owner. This difficulty is highlighted in sled dog racing, as at least eight feet always separates the driver from the nearest dog, with no leash attached. Furthermore, when running, the dog is looking away from and not toward the owner. From the first time the team is hooked up, control is at a distance and by voice only. Therefore, most obedience-trainers-turned-sled-dog-drivers find it more difficult to train an accurate, dependable sled dog than an accurate, dependable obedience dog.

SHOW DOGS
and SLED DOGS

Unlike show dogs, sled dogs do not have to be registered with any organization. No information about the dogs is requested on a race entry form. The only requirement for a sled dog is that he have a desire to run, the ability to do so, and that he be healthy. Any combination of breeds can be run on a single team.

Classes in racing, therefore, are not based on breed but rather on the maximum number of dogs on a team. Races can have a 3-dog, 4-dog, 6-dog, 8-dog, 10-dog maximum, and/or an unlimited class which has no maximum number of dogs. Distances vary with the class. The 3 dog class minimum distance each day is 3 miles; 4-dog class, 4 miles; 6-dog class, 6 miles; 8-dog class, 8 miles; and the 10-dog class, 10 miles. The Unlimited class minimums are 10 miles in December, 12 miles in January, and 15 miles until the end of the season.

While a show dog may compete in several classes at a show, a sled dog runs in only one class per race (although he may be entered in a short "Child's" race in addition to the regular race). If a race is a two day affair, one heat will be run each day. Only dogs and drivers which have run the first day may run the second day. The winner is the team having the best combined time.

Entry fees for small races range from $15.00 to $100.00, depending on the class and also the prize money involved.

Because the qualifications for a show dog and a sled dog are different, the champion of the show ring may never make a good sled dog; and the top sled dog of the season may never stand a chance in the show ring. There are, however, dogs that do compete in both shows and races and do well at both.

In the show ring, winning is based on the opinion of a judge and his interpretation of the breed standard. The "judge" in racing is the clock — the fastest time wins. Dogs may be checked by the Race Marshall/Chief Judge, but this is only to make sure they are fit to race and has no bearing on how they place.

TOM PALMER AND SIBERIANS
Registered show Siberians and a Doberman racing at Sisters, Oregon,
(Photo by "Mally" Hilands)

TRAINING THE JUNIOR MUSHER

Junior mushers come in a variety of sizes and ages — from the five-year-old who just stands on the runners while a trained leader pulls him 50 yards, to the 17-year-old who competently trains and drives a 7-dog team. For this discussion we are referring to a 10-year-old beginner. Adjust the instructions to fit the capabilities of your own child.

The first thing to determine is the degree of involvement your child really wants. If it is you who talks the child into a commitment, the results may be disastrous for all concerned. Be prepared for some commitment yourself.

If you are buying your first dog for the child, or if the dog you try to use turns out to be too active, untractable, snappy, lazy, or just too strong for your child, the most sensible thing to do is procure an older, reliable lead dog. An older dog can usually be found at a reasonable cost, particularly if it is going to a good home. The older dog will keep out of trouble himself and will be patient while your child is learning. Later on he can break in a younger dog much better than your child can. And most important of all, he can be depended upon to bring your child home safely.

Having gotten the new dog, or having allotted the child one of your own, give the child as much responsibility for caring for it as he is capable of assuming. Do not let the dog suffer because of the child's lack of maturity and the adult's lack of supervision. If you have dogs, let the child share in the care and feeding of all of them. The more animal handling experience the child has, the better his relationship with and understanding of his own dog will be.

During this period, if possible, let the child observe a team in action either from a vehicle behind the team or from the basket of the sled. An adult should explain to the child everything that is happeningand answer all questions he may have.

From the beginning teach the child how to set up and handle his equipment. He should get his own dog in and out of the dog truck, rig his own sled, harness and hook up his dog. He should untangle the dog when it gets in a mess. Don't play nursemaid, because when the child is on the trail, he will be on his own. On the other hand, give him enough instruction and encouragement so that he does not become discouraged.

If the child is starting with an untrained dog, the adult should take the dog up to the stage of controlled pulling in front of a moving vehicle with the child watching and helping where he can. When the child first gets on the vehicle, an adult should have a leash attached to the dog's collar for control. It is important that the dog not be allowed to bolt.

One dog is quite enough for a child to handle until he has become somewhat expert. If you eventually try two dogs in double lead, make certain the pair is compatible, as you do not want your child to have to cope with any unnecessary tangles or arguments.

Do not attempt too much at one time. Keep the runs short so as not to tire either dog or child. Keep the weight the dog has to pull to a minimum so that the child does not have to run too much. You do not want either child or dog to become discouraged at this early stage. If it has been a bad day, the child may need as much encouragement as the dog so that both of them will look forward to the next try.

TRAVELING WITH DOGS

Taking dogs on a trip means advance preparation. Dogs are not inanimate objects like an extra suitcase. Foresight is required for their welfare and for the protection of your property and that of others.

HOUSING

Some beginning mushers take their dogs loose in the family station wagon, but this is not an ideal arrangement. Dogs should have their own individual area where they can take the trip in comfort. It will be more convenient for you to carry your dogs in their own compartments; they like the security of their own place, and it is safer for the dogs and you. The wall of the compartment acts like a seat belt in case of a sudden stop, and the dog will not be thrown forward. Also during times when you are away from the vehicle, it is far better that there be no chance of a fight.

For these reasons, almost all mushers transport their dogs in individual boxes. Some are interior boxes anchored or built into a station wagon, van, camper or bus. Others are exterior boxes mounted on the bed of a truck or a trailer.

No matter what kind of compartment you use, make sure it has enough bedding to keep the dog warm. Straw has the best insulating qualities and is cheap. Water seeps to the bottom of the box while the top layer remains dry. Most dogs love to make a nest of it. Put in lots at the start of a trip and keep removing the wet bottom layer as you travel.

Watch the ventilation of the boxes as you travel. Small holes can be blocked in a snow storm. On a cold night they can ice over from the dogs' breath.

DOG BOXES
Randy Roe's dog boxes on and off truck. Alaskan husky Ring awaits
dinner from Naomi Roe. (Photos courtesy of Randy Roe)

ON THE ROAD

On any trip you can assume that you will want to stop,
stretch your legs, and relieve yourself. Your dogs will too —
but not necessarily at the same place. For the dogs, try for
some isolated but safe roadside turnout. Use common sense
about when to make your stops. Every six hours is a fair interval. Do it sooner if you've fed the dogs at the previous stop.
Some drivers of large teams, when on a journey of several
days, will let their dogs out only twice a day — morning and
night. At all times use consideration for others; unless out in
the unquestioned wilderness, *clean up the mess!*

A common problem for many drivers is traveling with a
dog that drools excessively. This is caused by nerves and can
be cured by taking the dog with you frequently on short
trips — even on errands around town — to accustom him to
traveling. In the meantime, carry plenty of towels.

Whenever you stop for any length of time on the road, turn
off your motor. You don't want your dogs to breathe the
fumes from the exhaust. Watch your own and other vehicles
at the race site particularly. It is perfectly all right to ask
someone parked near you to turn off his motor if its exhaust
is blowing in your dogs' faces.

DOG TRAILER

Doors are covered with metal grills. Storage compartment holds equipment. Shovels are attached to front and back of trailer. (Photos by Bob Levorsen)

SAMPLE CHECKLIST FOR TRAVELING

DOGS	PEOPLE	VEHICLE
General Equipment	boots, pads	battery jumper
can opener	drinks	catalytic heater
chains	first aid kit	fuel, matches,
coats	food	funnel
dog poop bag	gloves	flares
first aid kit	hair dryer	flashlights
food, canned	hats	knives
food, dry	jackets	pliers
leash	kleenex	screwdriver
medicines	maps-road and	shovel & pick for
oil (for snaps)	race site	digging out of
food pans	medicines	snowbank
shovels	Race instructions	starter fluid
spoon	money	tarp (to lie on while
straw	pillow	putting on chains
towels	rain gear	tire chains—extra
water bucket	sleeping bags	links

water containers
Racing Gear
chassis
dental floss, needle
   (for repairs)
dog bag
extra collars
extra snaps
harnesses
lines
rattlers
sleds
sled bags, mats
snow hooks
snub line
tape (for sled
   repairs)

socks
thermal under-
wear
thermos

tow cables
Windex
window scraper

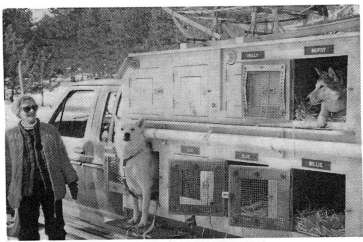

DOG TRUCK 1992 VERSION
Note flap dog is standing on. It helps dogs jump into their boxes;
folds up to cover the bottom of the doors; gives additional security;
and can be locked, securing all doors with one lock. Also, note
plastic tube for carrying extra runners, lights turned on separately
from headlights for night feeding, and thermal water carriers in rear
storage area.

TRAVELING EQUIPMENT

DOG TRUCK CHAINS

Dogs are attached to the vehicles that carry them by short chains with snaps at both ends. The chains need to be long enough so that the dog can eat from pans on the ground and lie down, but short enough so that two playful adjacent dogs cannot tangle their chains. Chains should also be short enough so that dogs cannot lunge out at passing children or dogs. It is better that the chains be short rather than too long.

Make provisions for hooking an appropriate number of chains to your truck, car and/or trailer by using eyebolts. Drill through your bumper, bumper support, and/or a suitable place along the side of the vehicle to provide a secure anchorage. Space the bolts far enough apart so that the chains don't meet. Make sure the snaps on the chains will go over the bolts.

STAKE OUT CHAIN

As an alternate procedure to chaining your dogs to your vehicle, and as a necessity when you have more dogs than eyebolts, you can use a stake out chain. This is a long, heavy chain which is stretched tight between trees or any solid objects. Short dog chains are permanently attached to the main chain. The snaps of the dog chains should not be able to meet by about a foot when the main chain is tight.

The ends of the main chain are extra long to go around large trees and then snap back onto the main chain. The end bolt snaps are extra large and strong.

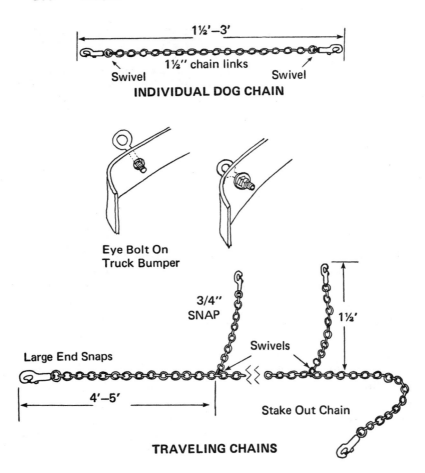

INDIVIDUAL DOG CHAIN

TRAVELING CHAINS

DOG BOXES
TRUCKS

The easiest design for building a set of dog boxes to be placed on the bed of a pickup truck involves a flat deck that spans across the pickup bed and projects on either side between 4 in. to 8 in. Allow for minimum inside box dimensions of 18 in. wide, 20 in. high and 30 in. deep. Variation of any dimensions up to 4 in. is all right. Boxes should be small enough so that the dogs can keep the boxes warm with their body heat in cold weather. The size of your boxes will depend somewhat on your climate and the size of your dogs. The dimensions given will comfortably accommodate a dog of 24 in. at the shoulders in northern California weather which frequently gets down to 10 degrees Fahrenheit at night.

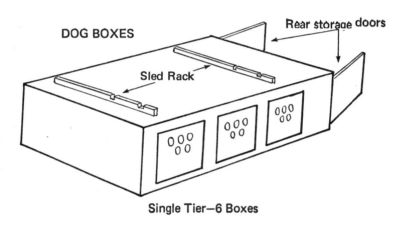

Single Tier—6 Boxes

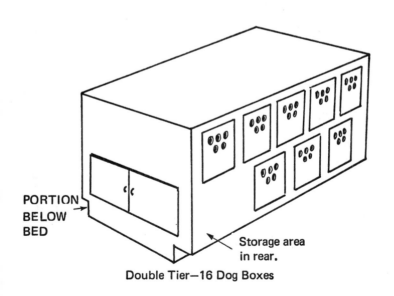

Double Tier—16 Dog Boxes

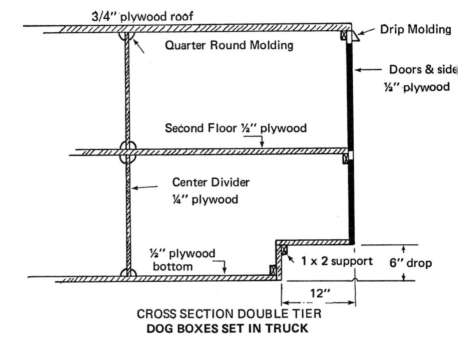

CROSS SECTION DOUBLE TIER
DOG BOXES SET IN TRUCK

TRAILERS

A trailer outfitted with either a single or double tier of boxes is often used. A trailer has the advantage that the family car can do the pulling. A trailer is also an answer for those using campers or motor homes.

A two axle trailer gives maximum stability. However, a single axle trailer is easier and lighter to maneuver when it must be detached from the vehicle so that it can be turned around in the small spaces that are often the only parking places available at a race site.

If you are going to buy a basic trailer and then convert it, a small utility or boat trailer with minimum wheels of 14 in. will provide a beginning. If you are going to build the trailer completely, it would be wise to have the advice of someone who is familiar with trailer construction.

ORGANIZATION
OF RACES

INTERNATIONAL SLED DOG RACING ASSOCIATION
The International Sled Dog Racing Association (ISDRA) was founded in 1966. It dedicates its activities to the sport of sled dog racing on a worldwide basis by standardizing race rules and race management procedures, by promoting public interest and driver education, and by encouraging cooperation among clubs.

ISDRA is governed at this writing by five at-large directors and thirteen regional directors. All directors are elected biannually by the membership. Any individual or organization interested in the sport can become a member of ISDRA by payment of dues.

ISDRA is a regulating body and does not put on races. Races are put on by the ever increasing number of individual sled dog clubs.

ISDRA rules were originally based on Alaskan rules. Most races either use them entirely or use them as a basis for their own rules. ISDRA sanctions some -   but not all   - races that meet its standards. Sanctioning is optional with the race giving organization. Sanctioned races earn points for some of the entrants toward medals and regional certificates.

The *ISDRA Officials Handbook* is a guide to procedures governing the duties of officials. Every serious driver would do well to study this handbook so that he will be prepared to serve in some official capacity when asked.

The *ISDRA Race Manual* provides guidance to clubs on all aspects of racing, including trail making, trail marking, publicity, sanctioning, and amateur status requirements.

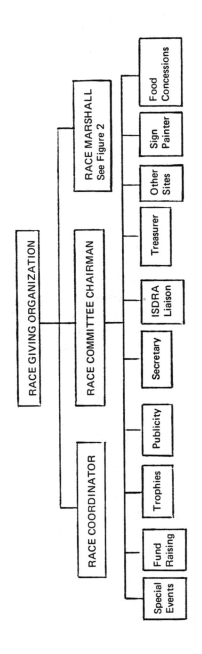

Figure 1. Chart showing relationship between the Race Giving Organization and its key officials.

Taken from the ISDRA OFFICIALS HANDBOOK

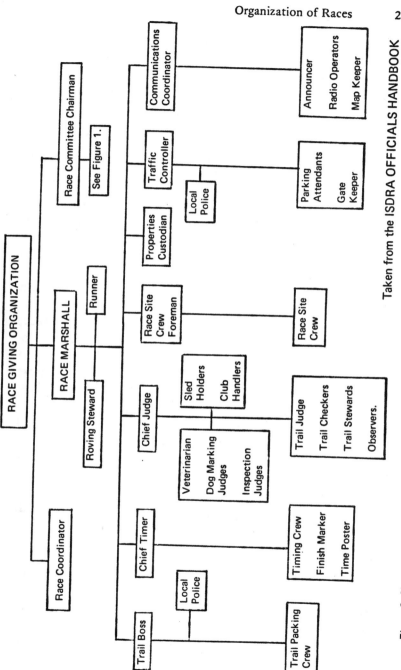

Taken from the ISDRA OFFICIALS HANDBOOK

Figure 2. Chart showing the relationship between the Race Marshall and his officials.

RACE GIVING ORGANIZATIONS

Many hours of planning and hard work are required to put on a race. Members of the organizing club must find a suitable race site, put in and maintain a trail, obtain sponsorship, assign officials, and arrange publicity. The number of jobs that are carried out for a major race and the relationship of the officials doing those jobs can be learned by study of the foregoing charts on the Organization of Races taken from the ISDRA *Officials Handbook*

RACE OFFICIALS

Every race, large or small, must have certain key officials in order to be a success. These are:

The *Race Marshall/Chief Judge* (some races divide the job between two people) is the person in complete charge of the entire race. He is appointed by the race giving organization and reports only to it. All other officials report to him. He is available for consultation during all phases of planning a race, and any questionable areas should have his approval. He decides the starting times for all classes and events and is in charge of the officials' meeting, drivers' meeting and Protest Committee. He is the only person who can disqualify a team, and he also has the power to cancel or stop a race due to weather or trail conditions. In short, he has final say on all matters, within the limits of the race rules.

The *Trail Boss* is responsible for the preparation and condition of the trail. He must know the requirements of a suitable trail and try to eliminate all hazards from the trail. He and his crew see to it that the trail is well packed, well marked, and that checkers and stewards are stationed at appropriate places.

The *Chief Timer* records the time it takes each team to run the course. He has assistants to help time, but he alone calls the countdown for each team leaving the chute.

The *Dog Marking Judge* marks each dog for identification so there can be no substitution of dogs. Different colors are used for the different classes. Markings are small, waterproof and harmless. One day races do not mark dogs.

STEWARDING

In addition to the major race officials, who are probably appointed before the beginning of the race season, the help of many other people is needed on the day of the race if the race is to run smoothly. These people can be those who manned the snowmobiles to pack the trail; dog drivers not running in that class or that race and members of their families; and sometimes, in a pinch, even casual spectators who are interested in taking part. The jobs these people do can be included in the following categories:

Trail Checkers' main function is to check off on a list each team as it passes and note any irregularities.

Trail Stewards are stationed by the Race Marshall at various places along the trail where drivers may need assistance.

Anyone on the trail may at some time find himself in a place where a team needs help. Assisting a team usually involves holding the sled while the driver untangles lines, leads his team into a turn, or perhaps changes the position of a dog. Once a team has left the starting line, only the driver is allowed to handle the dogs themselves if there is no emergency. An emergency is when any dog or driver is in danger of being hurt. A team running loose down the trail is definitely an emergency and any official or spectator is encouraged to stop it. In these emergency situations anyone may handle the dogs without the driver's being penalized.

Sled Holders are two or more men asked by the Race Marshall to hold each sled as it comes to the starting line so that the driver can go up to speak to his dogs. The sled is held by the stanchions until the driver is ready to go.

Club Handlers are those who help teams to the starting line. They can be officials appointed by the Race Marshall for the entire race, or they can be people who are not busy at the moment and are willing to help drivers who are short of handlers.

The job consists of asking drivers if they want help, then following their instructions. Usually the driver will want you to hold the main towline, keeping it at the level of the dogs' backs. Be alert for the driver's instructions; do *not* carry on loud conversations with friends. Watch the dogs for any chewing of lines. Sometimes the driver will ask you to carry the sled over a bare spot or to ride it while he takes the lead dog. When the team reaches the starting line it will be taken over by the sled holders, and you will be free to go back to help another team.

EUROPEAN SLED DOG RACING ASSOCIATION

The European Sled Dog Racing Association (ESDRA) is the counterpart in Europe to ISDRA. All its members are national sled dog racing organizations. It has rules for and sanctions two types of races. 1) the regular sled dog races held in North America, which they call Nome style racing, and 2) races where the driver is on skiis, and weight is carried either in a sled or inside a closed tobbogan-like carrier called a pulka, which they call Scandinavian style racing. ESDRA is responsible for the annual European Championship races held each year.

INTERNATIONAL FEDERATION OF SLEDDOG SPORTS

When ISDRA and ESDRA attempted to jointly apply for Olympic recognition from the International Olympic Committee, they were advised that only a single organization could make the application, in its capacity as the over-seeing organization for the sport worldwide. This necessitated the formation of a new organization in 1986 which was named the International Federation of Sleddog Sports (IFSS), with both ISDRA and ESDRA as Associate Members. National sled racing organizations become regular members on application.

IFSS is responsible for an annual international invitational sled dog event held among Olympic lines and called the IFSS World Championship Sled Dog Race, or the IFSS WC. Each country member sends teams to compete in as many of the classes as it wishes. Both Nome style and Scandinavian class races are held. Currently, the classes being raced are Unlimited, 8-dog, 6-dog and 4-dog Nome style classes, and Men's and Women's Pulka Scandinavian style classes. The Pulka classes have a three dog maximum, and usually race the 6-dog trail.

YOUR FIRST RACE

If you live more than four hours drive from the race site, you will probably want to arrive at the area the day before. This is advisable for several reasons: You can socialize with the other drivers, both to be friendly and to pick up useful tips. You and your dogs will be rested from the drive and will have more time to become used to any changed weather conditions. Also, you should be there in time for the drivers' meeting (sometimes held the night before the race) at which you will be briefed on the trail and other aspects of the race. Be sure to check your information sheet for time and place of this meeting.

On race day itself, get to the race site early, even if your class is not scheduled to go out until later in the day. There may be an updating of driver information, such as a change in the trail due to varying weather conditions. Also, at some races you might be needed to serve as trail checker for other classes or to help other drivers get to the starting chute. Remember, you may want their help when your turn comes.

A brief note here on small children: If you have children, they will be used to your dogs and so may approach other dogs with a lack of caution. Many sled dogs are kennel dogs not used to strangers, and even family dogs are high-strung at a race. So keep your children away from other dogs. Explain the situation to them, and then provide for their amusement elsewhere. Bring along toys suitable for their ages and local conditions. For infants, bring along front or back carriers.

As your race time approaches you will mentally check off last minute details. By now you should have studied the trail map, your dogs have probably been marked, and, hopefully, you have not forgotten where you left your race number. Check your equipment and make sure you have your dog bag, snowhook, and double-lead neckline. If you are parked any distance from the starting line, you will probably want help getting your team to it. Naturally, you thought this out in advance and don't have to run around frantically at the last minute looking for assistance.

Once in the holding line up, your sled will be inspected by an official to see that you are carrying the required equipment. The dogs, too, will be checked. A veterinarian may be on hand to advise the Race Marshall on a dog's fitness for the race. In the chute there will probably be someone to hold your sled. You should leave your sled to give each individual dog a few final words of encouragement. While you are talking to your dogs, don't forget to listen to the Chief Timer!

Back to the sled for the final 30 seconds of the countdown to the start, and then you are off and on your own. Whether across a frozen lake, on a narrow trail through pine woods, or up (and down) a snowed-over fire road, there is nothing quite like your first race. Enjoy it, but be thinking too. Try to remember the trail map and anticipate turns and possible problem areas. Be on the lookout for other teams, both oncoming and behind you. Remind yourself of the right of way rules on overtaking and passing. Try not to mix up 'Gee' and 'Haw' and be sure to identify all trail markers. Above all, always watch your dogs!

All too soon you will be across the finish line. In your excitement, don't forget to praise your dogs after they are well beyond the line. Back at your vehicle, unhitch them and if the weather is favorable, chain them up outside. After you have cared for your dogs, you will probably want to check your time on the posting board and exchange your trail experiences with other drivers. Don't relax too much though; there may be other classes that need your assistance.

After all racing is over and people are packing up to leave, you may want to slip on a pair of cross-country skis for a leisurely trek through the woods, or perhaps take turns giving your dogs short walks on a leash. Or you may prefer to go back to the motel to feed and water your dogs and enjoy a hot bath and cold beer before the mushers' banquet that evening. At the banquet there will be more talk and tale swapping, some eating and drinking, and lots of socializing.

Then comes the 10 p.m. "dog drop" which gives the dogs a last chance to relieve themselves and have a last drink of water.

The next morning you are back for another day of racing. By the time this day is over, perhaps a trophy or prize money will become one of your rewards. However, an even more memorable reward should be the exhilaration of an active weekend and getting to know new friends, as well as yourself and your dogs in a new context. Finally, you clean up your parking site, fill out your race report, bundle your dogs into your vehicle, and start for home — reliving this race as you drive and then planning for the next one.

FIRST RACE
Robyn Murer and her Malamutes Naklik and Kashak race at South Lake Tahoe, California, 1975.
Being marked for identification by Marking Judge Roxie Varvaro

Waiting in the lineup.

In the chute; sled held by Sue Field, dogs held by Lionel Talbot.

Away and running.
(Photos by Ed Murer)

HELPING ON THE TRIAL

Since bodies are always in short supply at a race, you are apt to be recruited by the Chief Checker to help on the trail. You can do this either before or after your class has run. If you go out before your class, request that you be brought back in time to get your dogs ready to run. The instructions for "Checkers" in the Appendix tells you what to do when you are a checker, and it gives you an idea of what you can expect from the checkers on the trail when you are racing in your class.

WEIGHT PULLING

Much of the information in this chapter was taken from "NDN Seminar on WEIGHT PULLING", Northern Dog News, November, 1973, with panelists Merle Mays, Kay and Ed Rodewald, John and Maxene Ramey, and Howard Baron, Chairman of the ISDRA Weight Pulling Committee.

Weight pulling is a fascinating hobby for owners who have dogs that are too large to be good racers. It has certain advantages over racing in that only one dog need be kept, training can be exclusively in the owner's backyard, and the owner himself does not have to be as athletically inclined as the racing driver. While weight pulling contests are not held with as much frequency as races, champion weight pulling dogs can become as well known as outstanding racing leaders.

Some outstanding weight pullers are: Champion Traleika of Tundra, a Malamute owned by Kay and Ed Rodewald of Oregon. Traleika's best pull was 2,060 pounds at Sisters, Oregon in 1974. Count Baranof of Kent, a Samoyed owned by John and Maxene Ramey of Washington, went undefeated for four seasons. His best pull was in 1970 at Sisters, Oregon where he pulled 2,205 pounds.

That same year at the North American Championship in Fairbanks, Alaska, a female Malamute named Tearaleste Nake Neiu, owned by Roger Burggraf, pulled 2,200 pounds.

Howard Baron's Malamute, Lobo, from Southern California was undefeated in his several years of campaigning all up and down the west coast of the United States and Canada. His greatest feat was pulling a truck and trailer — a weight of 10,000 pounds — on a level, paved road. Even after Lobo's retirement, Howard says, "He can break a ½ in. piece of sisal rope on command and has broken a 650 pound test nylon rope on command. . .He has broken everything except extra heavy steel snaps."

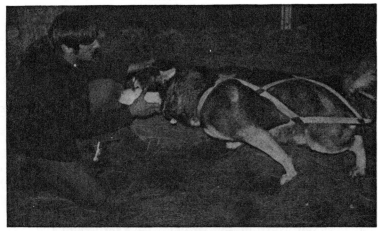

HOWARD BARON AND LOBO
AND THE WEIGHT LOBO IS PULLING
(Photos courtesy of Howard Baron)

TYPES OF DOGS

Weight pulling dogs are usually larger and heavier boned than racing dogs. One of the most popular purebreds entered in this event is the Alaskan Malamute. However, any dog regardless of breed or sex can compete.

A great deal of importance is placed on the dog's conformation. The dog should be well balanced and have strong hind quarters. Any unsoundness will adversely affect the dog's ability to pull.

Conditioning and physical fitness are as important to this sport as to any other athletic event, so a weight puller must be given regular exercise and a limited amount of good food.

Temperament also plays a major role. Shy dogs may become frightened or confused by the people and noise at a competition. On the other hand, the overtly aggressive dog may spend more time trying to fight than to work. When starting to train a weight puller, you should make an honest evaluation of your dog's physical ability and his potential and not expect more than the dog is capable of doing.

EQUIPMENT
HARNESS

The harness is the most important piece of equipment involved. The Siwash harness is the most popular type used, although the old-fashioned freighting harness with a round leather collar is sometimes used. The Siwash has padded chest and shoulder straps at points of stress—as does a racing harness —and pull is evenly distributed. Unlike the racing harness, it has a spreader bar placed horizontally behind the dog's rear legs, preventing the side straps from rubbing against the dog's legs or confining his movements.

Make certain your dog has a properly fitted harness at all times. "The chest portion must not restrict his breathing by riding up and pressing on his windpipe. The neck and shoulders should fit snugly without binding or restricting movement." (Gail Ferguson, et. al., *Mile-Hi Musher,* Vol. 12, Rocky Mountain Sled Dog Club, Denver, 1975)

Often you may need two harnesses for your grown dog,

one for summer when his coat is thin, and the other for winter when his full coat adds considerably to his overall dimensions.

LOAD
Many different kinds of weights have been used for training.
Logs, tires, carts, wagons, sleds, drags, or boxes filled with
rocks or bricks have all been used. Whatever load you use, be
sure not to allow any of it to hit the dog's rear legs.

"It is a good idea to test the weight of the load yourself,
especially in working with young dogs, since friction varies
greatly according to the surface and type of load involved."
(Ferguson, *op, cit.*)

TRAINING
AGE OF DOG
The training of a weight puller should start at an early age
if possible. Many trainers begin as early as three months, but
training at this stage is a socializing process. Basic formal
training usually starts at about six months. An early start accustoms the dog to the harness and noise. As in all kinds of
training, young dogs tend to be more responsive and easier to
train than older ones.

WEIGHT USED
Since the large breeds do not usually reach physical maturity until at least 18 months, you should begin with light
loads and work up gradually to heavier ones. For example,
start with 25 pounds and add 25 pounds as you condition
your dog. Never add more than 50 pounds of new weight at a
time. Make sure you never put a strain on your young dog.

POSITION OF TRAINER
To get your dog to pull you can stand either back from him
and call your dog from the front, or you can stand at his
shoulder and drive him from the rear. Although the latter
method may seem harder, it is preferred because it is more
professional and the pulling becomes more of a team effort

between you and your dog. Changing your position can be confusing to your dog, so right from the beginning decide where you are going to stand. Check local competition rules. - ISDRA rules require standing behind the dog's shoulder.

BEGINNING TRAINING

The first step is to hook a small weight to the tugline of the harness and urge the dog to pull it around the yard for a short period of time. The amount of time that the weight is attached should increase up to an hour or more each day as the dog matures and becomes accustomed to the weight and the noise. During these weight-dragging sessions, encourage the dog with attention and praise. Always keep in mind that the sessions should be fun and never boring to the dog. Remember that the attitude of the dog is an important factor in successful weight pulling. Patience on the part of the trainer is equally important. These play-work sessions will help you gain your dog's respect and confidence.

Once the dog is accustomed to the harness and pulling, put a leash or long line on the dog's collar and give a 'Hike!' command—or whatever your go command will be to the dog as you run around the yard.

INTERMEDIATE TRAINING

If you are going to drive your dog from the shoulder, the next step is to get him to move out in front of you on command. One of the easiest and best methods is to run a cord or rope around a strong post or tree. One end is attached to the dog's collar and the other is held in your hands. As you give your forward command, at the same time pull the cord in quick, short jerks. This pulling enables you to move the dog forward while you remain behind him; but while he is moving, walk forward with him. Have him go at least 20 feet and then give him a command to stop.

If you are going to call your dog from the front, pull him from the front with the same quick jerks as you walk backwards. Eventually increase the distance you are standing from him to at least 20 feet and pull him in to you.

Your dog's pulling should be done in a continuous move-ment. Never allow him to jump and leap about or stop and sniff his surroundings. Also, he should pull in a straight line. The continuous pull will conserve his energy and also prevent him from harming himself.

Because of the mechanics of his build, your dog must have his head down to pull. So whether you stand in front or along-side of him, crouch down so that he can see you without rais-ing his head. Once the dog starts to pull, you should praise him constantly.

When you have taught your dog what is expected of him, he must always finish his pull. Never give in or allow him to stop half way. If for some reason he cannot pull the weight ex-pected of him, you must assist him so he will not become dis-couraged. Every training session should end on a happy note, no matter how small the progress.

TEAM PULLS

In many areas, a popular variation of the one dog pull is having two or three dogs work together as a team to pull the weight. The dogs are trained and conditioned as individuals and then taught to work together.

If two dogs are used, they may be harnessed next to one another in double lead. Or they may be hooked one behind the other, usually with the larger, stronger dog in the wheel position. When three or more dogs are used, the stronger dogs are always in wheel.

Learning to pull in unison is the most important point of this team effort and is achieved only by extensive training.

WEIGHT PULLING CONTESTS

Weight pulling contests are usually held in conjunction with regular races. They are great crowd pleasers. If you wish to enter one, check the information sheet of your chosen race to see if a weight pull is included and what classes are being held.

Except for multiple dog pulls, the classes offered are usual-ly a) dogs weighing 65 pounds or less, b) dogs weighing over 65 pounds and up to 125 pounds, c) dogs over 125 pounds.

CH. TRALEIKA OF TUNDRA
Pulling weights at Granby, Colorado.
(Photo courtesy of Kay and Ed Rodewald)

JOHN RAMEY AND COUNT BARANOF OF KENT
(Photo copy from Northern Dog News, with permission by Mark Levorsen)
Original photo by "Mally" Hilands

The dog has 90 seconds to pull the load a distance of 20 feet.

The dogs entered take turns pulling a specific weight. After the completion of each round of pulls, more weight is added. Dogs are eliminated as they can't complete the pull until only one dog is left. This dog is the winner of his class.

FREIGHT RACES

Freight racing is a cross between weight pulling and regular racing. The weight pulling type dog and the weight pulling harness are usually used, but the drag or heavy freight-type sled is replaced by an extra strong racing sled. About 40 pounds of weight (usually sand bags) for each dog in the team is added to the sled.

The classes of the teams are determined by the number of dogs run. Distances run are shorter than the regular races because of the weight being carried. They can be anything from a few hundred yards to a few miles. Freight races are especially fun for spectators to watch.

PULKA RACING
Scandinavian style racing, very popular in Europe, where the musher is on skiis and attached to a small, toboggan-like "Pulka" in which weight is carried. Here, Josef Niedermeier of Germany starts off with his two purebred Siberians on a 6 mile trail at Bad Mitterndorf, Austria during the 1992 IFSS World Championships. (Photo by Bob Levorsen).

SUMMER BACKPACKING

By *Malin Foster of Logan, Utah, a free-lance writer and professional guide for wilderness backpackers, with assists from Jim Mitchell of Nordkyn Outfitters, P.O. Box 158, Pullman Washington 99163 and Dave Chenette of Wenaha Dog Packs, P.O. Box 2081 Lynnwood, Washington 98036.*

Increased interest in the wilderness is sending more and more folks into the outback with loads on their backs. Dogs have been carrying loads for man for uncounted years, so there is no reason why the family pet can't be of service now in a recreational sense.

DAVE CHENETTE AND KODI
"...one of the best pack dogs I have ever had."
(Photo courtesy of Dave Chenette)

THE DOG

For carrying a pack, the dog should be medium to large in size and must be tall enough to keep his pack from hitting every rock in the trail. Working dogs with a steady disposition are usually the most satisfactory type.

If the dog does not automatically stay with the owner, he must be trained somewhat differently than the usual sled dog. Obedience training is closer to the mark. If the dog is to be turned loose with a pack on his back, he must be infallibly trained to 'Whoa' or to 'Come' on command; but it is asking a lot of even the most well trained dog to cease chasing a deer on verbal command. On lead, the dog must be trained not to pull or lunge, as such behavior can be extremely tiring and frustrating to a hiker trying to negotiate a rough trail with a heavy pack on his own back.

THE PACK

A variety of professional packs can be purchased from the dog equipment firms mentioned above, from certain sporting goods or mountain equipment shops, or a simple pack can be made at home.

In general, the pack consists of two bags, or panniers, one for each side of the dog, fastened together at the top by a broad band of fabric to distribute the load. If the panniers were held together by straps, the weight would be concentrated too much.

The pack should be constructed so that it rides comfortably on the shoulders and upper back where the muscular and skeletal structure of the dog is the strongest. A loaded pack should never be placed so that it bears down on the center of the dog's back.

The panniers should be deep enough to keep the weight well down on the dog's sides so that he can keep his balance. The bottom of the pack should be about even with the dog's belly.

Nylon pack cloth is the material generally used, although canvas or even burlap can be used. Good packs have additional tough material sewn to the bottom half of both panniers to

SADDLE
(with bags removed)

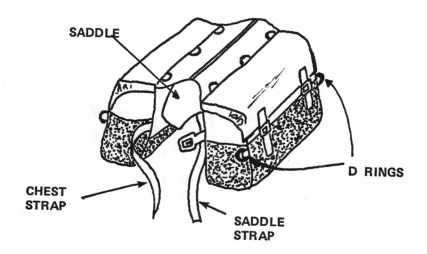

DOG PACK

WRAP—AROUND STRAP
Malin Foster attaching strap to his dog's pack.
(Photo courtesy of Malin Foster)

take the beating of rocks and brush, because with all its lightness and water repellent qualities, nylon does not stand abrasion well.

The method of holding the pack on with straps differs somewhat with the construction of the individual pack. In general, the pack should have one strap that goes around the front of the chest to hold the panniers in and forward, one that goes under the rib cage, and one that joins the backs of the two panniers together by passing under the dog's belly. No strap goes around the dog's rear. Buckles are often padded for extra protection. Last of all, every pack should have a separate 11 foot wrap-around strap which is helpful in reducing the bulk of the pack and holding it firmly to the dog. This strap is useful during mountain travel but is not necessary for training or for short hikes in level, non-brushy areas.

TRAINING

The dog should be introduced to his new gear gently and gradually. Put the pack on without anything in it at first to accustom the dog to having a pack on his back. After short sessions he can graduate to a light, bulky load of wadded newspapers to get the feel of the swing and bulk of the pack. Take him for short walks with the light pack, and then increase the weight and distance gradually until the dog is used to carrying a load. Having the dog carry supplies for a picnic makes a nice afternoon outing for both of you.

WEIGHT

As a general rule, a mature dog in good condition who is used to packing can comfortably carry 1/3 of his total body weight. For early training, ¼ of the dog's body weight is suitable. A young dog should carry less than a mature one of 18 months to 2 years. Condition is the key. Adjust the weight your dog carries to his age, strength and experience.

BALANCE

The weight of the pack must be distributed evenly and must be balanced both fore and aft and on both sides. At home, the contents for each side can be weighed on a scale. In the field, just slipping the pack on the dog without cinching up will generally show if the panniers are unbalanced.

CONTENTS

Let the dogs carry items which will not suffer getting wet: small stoves, gas cans, tarps, tightly sealed food bottles, etc. No matter how well trained, some dogs will insist on wading into whatever water is available. It cools them off. Sometimes they must get wet when fording a stream. A dog with a loaded pack usually won't venture into water that is too deep; but if there is any question about the depth or footing of a stream that must be crossed, take the pack off the dog.

Consult your veterinarian for first aid supplies to take along for your dog as needs differ from area to area. For example, some places don't have snakes; others do. In porcupine country, a good pair of needle-nosed pliers is a must. Dog boots don't weigh much and are good to have in case of emergency.

Avoid objects with sharp corners. If there is any question of an object's being uncomfortable, the dog's body should be protected by a sweater or some other soft material placed inside the pack between the object and the dog.

D rings attached to the yolk of the pack make it possible to tie on a small tent or tarp.

Don't put your own survival gear in the dog's pack, as there is always a chance that you will become separated from your dog.

After traveling a short distance, readjust straps. If the dog shows any discomfort, check for problems.

FEEDING

Do not feed a dog heavily before starting a trip. On the trail feed at night or when making camp. Dogs often will eat a bit less than usual on the first night; but if the dog wants to eat, he should be given full, normal rations, or even a little extra because he is working. A well conditioned dog can do a couple of days' packing without eating anything, but after that he must have nourishment.

TRAIL MANNERS

Good sense is your best guide, but trail manners require that a pack dog either be trained to stay with you or be kept on a leash. In much of the national forest back country, grazing permits are still valid, and backpackers will encounter sheep and range cattle. Sheep-chasing dogs get shot. So do cattle chasers. Even if no wrangler is with the cattle, as is often the case, an irate range cow can wipe out a dog with her hoof.

Remember that other people on wilderness trails and in camps may not like to have a friendly husky dish out an enthusiastic greeting. Also, never allow your dog to harass wildlife, as many of them will if given the chance. Keep your dog restrained and it will not get itself or you into trouble. The kind of restraint depends largely upon the dog, but a suitable chain or metal cable leash is a worthwhile and necessary investment in space and weight.

REGULATIONS

The National Park Service has a definite rule about dogs in national parks: none may be taken on back country trails—anywhere. It is a new rule and is universal.

The U. S. Forest Service may have individual restrictions here and there, but generally dogs under control are welcome. Other agencies, such as the U. S. Bureau of Land Management share the Forest Service's attitude about dogs. If there is any question as to regulations, check before you start.

Have a good outing!

WINTER CAMPING

Dogs are most helpful to the winter wilderness camper, and the family pet who has been trained to pull a load on a sled will be a great addition to his snow country outing.

Malamutes are particularly suited to this form of recreation because they have a natural willingness to work, have the strength to pull a load, do not get frustrated if they must go slowly, and they like to spend the night curled up in the snow.

For a harness, use the regular racing harness if you have one or the weight pulling type if you are making one up especially for this purpose.

Use a sturdily constructed, but not heavy sled. Remember that many sleds not much heavier than a racing sled have traveled the thousand mile Iditarod race trail from Anchorage to Nome. The main point about the sled is that it should have a long enough basket to stow all of your gear.

A regulation hardwood toboggan can be used as a freighting sled. It weighs about 40 pounds and is easy for a large dog to pull. Of course, it would be suitable for only certain trails, and the musher would have to be on skis or snowshoes.

Be sure to pack your gear with a tarp over it to hold the pieces together and to keep snow from getting into everything. Tie the load down well so that it won't come off in case the sled or toboggan overturns.

Happy camping!

SKIJOURING

Skijoring consists basically of having a dog pull a cross country skier instead of a sled. To make this a successful enterprise, the skier should first be competent on his skis. Second, the dog should be steady at pulling and should know the rudiments of commands. This is not a place for both skier and dog to learn together.

Use a racing type harness with and 8 — 10 foot towline. Attach a trapeze-shaped handhold for the skier. If more than one dog is to be used, they can be hitched in pairs or single file. Don't take more dogs than you can handle. Give your dog the command to go and then proceed as if cross country skiing.

A refinement of the sport is to have either the dog or the skier or both carry light, loaded packs on their backs.

Good luck and bon voyage!

SKIJOURING
Racing with three dogs abreast pulling a musher on skis with no brakes requires both a good skier and well trained sled dogs. (Photo by Bob Levorsen).

PARASITES

The following sections on parasites, diseases, health problems and nutrition were written by Corey Cherrstrom, D.V.M., a recent graduate of the University of California Veterinary College at Davis. Dr. Cherrstrom is also a sled dog driver.

For the 1980 edition of MUSH, all of the book was reviewed and suggestions for these sections were made by Roland Lombard, D.V.M., world champion sled dog driver from Wayland, Massachusetts.

Dogs that have internal parasites cannot give the best performance on a sled dog team of which they are capable. They can be thin, weaker than normal, have a bad coat, and, at best, need extra food.

The first step in eliminating parasites is to have your dogs checked regularly by your veterinarian. Any new dog should be immediately checked. Adult dogs already in your kennel should be checked at least once a year. Never give worming medicine without a check by your veterinarian first. Worming is a science, not a guessing game. You must give the right medicine in the proper dosage for each specific type of worm.

Collect a small fecal sample from each dog. The sample should be fresh and from a well-formed part of the stool. Put it in a glass or plastic container for easy removal by the veterinarian. (Baby food jars and margarine tubs are good.) Write the dog's name on the container. Your vet should also know where the dog came from so that he can check for worms peculiar to that area. If you can't get the sample to the vet immediately, keep it where it will neither get too hot nor freeze. Samples will be usable for about 24 hours after collection if refrigerated. One negative sample does not necessarily mean that the dog does not have worms. To be absolutely sure, three or four samples taken at different times should be checked

Fleas carry parasites. Unfortunately, they are adaptable and all too quickly build up resistence to any specific chemical, so the chemical used to eliminate them must be changed periodically.

Flea collars work well if the type of active chemical is changed every so often. Several good flea soaps are available, but frequent use is not recommended because washing removes the oil from the skin and makes it dry and itchy. Some sprays and powders work well. The chemical "malathion", when used according to directions, is good for clearing up infestation in the kennel or yard, and even in your home. Commercial foggers also work in a closed area. Be prepared to repeat the treatment in 30 days when the flea reproduction starts to repeat.

In recent years more dogs have been traveling across the country, and heartworm has been traveling with them. Now, any area that has mosquitoes and not a long and cold enough winter to keep them in check, has a problem. The symptoms of heartworm are few at first, so the only reliable way to tell if your dog is infected is to have him checked by a veterinarian. A preventive medicine is available which many people give to their dogs throughout the mosquito season. But before it is given, every dog MUST BE CHECKED BY A VETERINARIAN to find out whether or not it already has heartworm. To give the preventive medicine to an infected dog can kill him.

To keep parasites in general down, the dog's bedding and living area should be kept as clean and dry as possible. Most parasites and mosquitoes have trouble living in a dry area. A kennel design which gives good drainage to allow thorough cleaning and to prevent standing water is essential.

To be safe, cook all fish, meat and bones that do not come from the grocery store.

If worms are a persistent problem, sometimes it is best to move the entire kennel and then treat the contaminated area with a flame thrower or strong disinfectant. Spreading non-caustic lime on the ground keeps down hookworm. A black light with an electrified wire mesh around it will attract and kill mosquitoes. The units are expensive, but work well.

DISEASES

Puppies should be taken to the veterinarian at about eight weeks of age for the first vaccination against distemper, hepatitis and leptospirosis. The general program followed by most veterinarians is a series of between two and four vaccinations, with the first given at the first visit and the last given between the 14th and 16th weeks.

Most veterinarians recommend a yearly booster shot for adult dogs. For racing dogs, this shot is usually given several weeks before the racing season begins to give the dogs immunity from anything they may pick up during travel or from other teams.

Vaccination of one's own dogs is not recommended as these vaccines are somewhat unstable unless kept refrigerated, and most good quality vaccines are sold only to graduate veterinarians.

CANINE COUGH

This disease is caused by a virus and is highly contagious between dogs. It affects the upper airways and results in a pronounced cough that seems as if the dog has something caught in his throat.

In light cases the only treatment necessary is calming the cough and breaking down the thick mucus in the throat. Robitussin works well.

In severe cases, particularly when the temperature becomes elevated, a veterinarian should be seen. Precaution against secondary infection will probably be given.

Prevention is by keeping well dogs separated from infected

ones and by a new vaccine. Unless the dogs are vaccinated, when one dog in a kennel comes down with this cough, usually all the dogs get it one after another. The parainfluenza vaccine for canine cough now can come included in the regular distemper-hepatitis-leptospirosis vaccine. Since canine cough is so common and so contagious, it is recommended that you include the parainfluenza vaccine in your yearly booster.

A dog should probably be rested three or four days after the cough subsides before it is returned to training. Any dog with canine cough should not be taken to a race site.

PARVO

A deadly disease to which puppies are particularly susceptible. See your veterinarian for early vaccination.

HEALTH PROBLEMS

APPETITE LOSS (Anorexia)

Loss of appetite may be due to a variety of things: unhealthy dog, pain, hot weather, disagreeable food. First, try to decide the cause. If the problem is severe, seek professional advice. A sled dog in training or racing should not go more than one or two days without eating.

BLOAT (Gastric Torsion and/or Dilation)

When this condition occurs, it is after the dog eats dry or semi-moist food, drinks water, and then exercises. Sometimes exercise is not a necessary ingredient. What happens is that both the opening into the stomach and the exit from it become blocked. In torsion, the stomach actually twists on itself. In dilation, the dry food swells excessively from absorbing water. In both cases the gas produced by the food cannot escape and causes a ballooning of the front portion of the abdomen and the rear portion of the chest. Shock and death follow if the condition is not relieved. The time sequence of these events varies from 1 to 12 hours, depending on the severity of the case, with torsion being more serious than dilation.

This is an emergency situation. Once the signs begin, time is critical. Get the dog to the veterinarian as fast as possible, anytime of day or night. An immediate operation is often necessary.

CONSTIPATION

If a dog has not had a bowel movement for several days, a child's dosage of laxative, an enema, or suppositories may be given.

Dog Drivers often give suppositories before a race to prevent mid-race slowdowns. This may be done about an hour before race time.

CUTS (Lacerations)

Excessive bleeding must be stopped as soon as possible. Applying a bandage with direct pressure from your hand over the wound is best. Using a tourniquet is all right, but it must be loosened every 10–15 minutes.

For bad cuts, see a veterinarian as soon as possible. For minor ones, clip the hair around the wound, clean with mild soap or peroxide, apply an antibiotic ointment, cover with gauze, and tape. If taping around a leg, watch for swelling below the taped area. If this occurs, loosen the tape.

DEHYDRATION

This condition is hard to diagnose in a dog and is best done by pulling on the skin and seeing how fast it recoils. The skin loses elasticity in proportion to the amount of dehydration. The eyes and mouth may also be dry. Give the dog lukewarm, not cold, water. If the dog does not want to drink, tempt him by adding to the water a small amount of dog food or anything else that tastes good. If dehydration is serious and the dog will not drink, fluids must be given intravenously.

Sled dog drivers try to make sure that their dogs drink enough water so that they won't bite snow during a run.

DIARRHEA

Fresh blood and mucus in the stool and diarrhea are the usual signs of a problem in the large intestine that should be investigated by a veterinarian.

Occasionally diarrhea, with or without blood, will be seen during or following a long run or a race. The exact cause is not known, but usually the condition is not severe or prolonged enough to be given treatment.

Diarrhea can occur during travel from anxiety and/or excitement.

Loose stools can be caused by mixing too much water with dry food or by changing the food brand too rapidly.

Treatment of diarrhea is a) 1 2 tablespoons of Kaopectate per 50 pounds every 6–8 hours, b) bland diet of raw hamburger, rice and cottage cheese. If condition is frequent or persists, see your vet.

FEET

Feet are a trouble area in sled dogs. The normal feet on running dogs are tough but smooth, occasionally with superficial, but not deep, cracks.

Cut or worn feet need protection in the form of bandaging and/or dog boots. Rest from running is advised to insure uncomplicated healing. Compounds like Kopertox to toughen the feet may speed up the healing.

Blisters, usually from running a long distance on a hard surface, take time to heal. If they are open, they need to be kept clean and protected.

Snowballs may collect between the toes of dogs if snow conditions are right. Usually the dog shows sudden lameness while running. Pull them out as soon as possible. Vaseline petroleum jelly rubbed between the toes before the run will help prevent snowballs.

HEAT PROSTRATION

This condition occurs when a dog works too hard for the weather. It can also occur when a dog is left in a parked car and the inside temperature rises much higher than the outside temperature. Heat prostration can also occur when a dog is just tied to his house. Any air temperature over 90 degrees is cause for concern.

Symptoms of heat prostration are: heavy panting; eyes seem glassy; the dog can stand stiffly with his feet propped out like a saw horse; or he can collapse and fall down. He will be in obvious distress, or even unconscious. You have only a few minutes to cool him down before he suffers permanent damage, or even dies. Douse him with water all over. Make sure the water gets down to his skin. If a lake is nearby, submerge him and get in with him. If he starts to act more normal in a few minutes, he will be all right. If he does not, get him to a veterinarian immediately. Take care that his body temperature is not cooled below normal.

HYPOGLYCEMIA (Low Blood Sugar)

This condition will be seen during or after heavy training or a strenuous race. It is due to the body having inadequate stores of energy or the inability of the body to use the energy already stored. The signs are weakness, disorientation, and possibly muscle tremors. Treatment consists of giving a concentrated source of energy: Karo syrup, 2 tablespoons per 50 pounds.

MUSCLE PULLS

Ice the area for a few hours if the injury is detected during the first 24 hours, DMSO, available from your veterinarian, works well for sprains and muscle pulls.

Dogs with such injuries should be rested for several days. Walk them first, and then run them off the team to see if they are all right before returning them to the team.

POISONING

Determine what the poison is, if possible. If it is not caustic, induce vomiting by giving a) two or three tablespoons of hydrogen peroxide or b) a child's dose of Ipecac. If the dog is having convulsions or is not totally conscious, don't give anything. Call a veterinarian or take the dog to his office.

RECOVERING FROM LAMENESS OR ILLNESS

For lameness, refrain from hard training for about a week, depending on the severity of the injury. Run the dog next to a bicycle, car or sled for a few days to build him up before returning him to the team.

A good rule of thumb for illnesses is to let the dog rest for the same number of days that he has been sick before starting training again.

Every case must be handled individually. Get advice from your veterinarian and use common sense.

SHOCK

Shock may occur after trauma: car accident, extensive bleeding in a short period, dog fight, over exertion, and a variety of diseases. Signs are shallow, rapid respiration (normal rate is 10–30 times per minute at rest); rapid heart rate (normal is 80–120); weak pulse (taken at middle of inside thigh); and poor circulation. To check circulation, press on the gums and see if the return of color is prolonged.

Keep the dog warm and quiet and get him to the vet as soon as possible.

VOMITING

Vomiting is the primary sign of stomach irritation. Sometimes it happens on an empty stomach because of hyperacidity, which is probably due to a nervous condition. If vomiting is short term, it is usually insignificant and nothing to worry about. If it is persistent, either of sudden onset or over a long period, it usually indicates a serious problem which requires veterinary attention.

FIRST AID KIT FOR DOGS

1. *Antibiotic ointment* – for open wounds.
2. *Antibiotic pills* – for puncture wounds.
3. *Aspirin* – for pain. Dose: one tablet per 50 pounds every four to six hours. Give with food.
4. *Cotton*
5. *Gauze*
6. *Hydrogen Peroxide* – to induce vomiting, two tablespoons orally. To clean wounds, apply locally.
7. *Icthammal ointment, Numotizine, or DMSO* – for reducing swelling associated with muscle, tendon or ligament damage. Use after ice packing.
8. *Ipecac* – to induce vomiting after poisoning. Dose: one tablespoon orally for 50 pound dog.
9. *Kaopectate* – for diarrhea. Dose: one to two tablespoons per 50 pounds every six to eight hours.

10. *Kopertox* — for toughening and healing feet. Basic ingredient, tannic acid.
11. *Karo Syrup* — for hypoglycemia. Dose: two tablespoons usually enough.
12. *Nail clippers*
13. *Pepto Bismol* — to coat stomach and neutralize contents. Dose: child's dose.
14. *Scissors*
15. *Soap*
16. *Suppositories* — for constipation.
17. *Tape*
18. *Thermometer*
19. *Tweezers*
20. *Vaseline* — for preventing snowballs.

NUTRITION

The sled dog is a unique animal in regard to feeding since he expends a great deal of energy in a relatively short period of time. This energy must be replaced daily to assure good performance. When not in training, sled dogs can be maintained on most of the name brand commercial foods.

When in training and racing, it has been recently shown by Dr. Kronfeld, an expert on nutrition, that a food in which energy is derived from a proportion of predominantly protein and fat, with carbohydrates contributing less than 20%, may be best. This fact was also shown in food tests on sled dogs in the Antarctic years ago.

Dr. Kronfeld found the best diet to contain chicken and chicken parts fortified with the necessary vitamins and minerals. Drivers on the 1,049 mile Iditarod race found that beaver meat worked well. The traditional fish and rice, and sometimes tallow, combination of the Alaskan Indians has always been successful. For most sled dog drivers, however, the feeding of a good grade commercial dry dog food with the addition of a small amount of meat, meat by-products and fats, and/or cooking oil will probably provide an adequate diet for their purposes. Make sure the fat is not spoiled or the oil rancid. Check the label on your dog food for its contents.

Many vitamin supplements are available that may be good to add to the food. The main thing is not to overdo it; just because a little is good, a lot is not better. It is known that over-feeding of several of the vitamins and minerals will cause serious, often irreversible diseases in dogs. Usually the amount of vitamins already in a good commercial food is sufficient.

When changes are made in a dog's diet, make them gradually over a 3—4 day period to prevent upsetting his intestinal tract. Adding too much water to dry food may make his stool loose.

Sled dogs need an increase in the amount of food given to them to keep up with the increased demands on their energy as training progresses and the miles run get longer. If increasing the amount of food causes your dog to develop diarrhea or a stool containing undigested food, it may be that he is being fed too much at one time. Try dividing his ration into two feedings a day.

To determine if your dog's diet is adequate, several things must be watched. The dog should be checked about weekly to make sure that his weight is maintained but that he is not getting fat. You should always be able to feel his ribs easily right under his skin. The dog should look healthy as well as feel good. Hair coat can be a guideline for adequate diet since hair, as well as the rest of the body, needs a balanced diet for normal health. Hair should be shiny and lie more or less flat, depending on the breed. It should never be dry and brittle.

In above freezing temperatures, water should always be available and should be changed daily. In freezing weather and when on the road, sled dogs are usually watered twice a day with warm water to which has been added some "bait" in the form of ground meat or canned dog or cat food to encourage drinking.

SAFETY ON THE TRAIL
The Importance of ISDRA Race Rules

When you watch a team go out the starting chute at a race it usually looks pretty simple and goes off without a hitch. How does the transformation from the chaotic scene in the staging area become a safe race and how does it stay that way? It all begins with the International Sled Dog Racing Association (ISDRA) Race Rules.

Race rules which promote animal welfare are nothing new to sled dog racing. Since the first major organized race in 1909 (The All Alaska Sweepstakes in Nome, Alaska), race rules have been implemented to safeguard dogs and mushers alike. ISDRA sanctioned races must comply with ISDRA's rules and regulations which dictate everything from trail length and layout to mandatory safety equipment to canine fitness.

In order to become an ISDRA sanctioned race, the race course must comply with detailed trail requirements. The basic premises governing trail design all concern safety.

- The trail must not endanger dog teams or drivers.

- All avoidable hazards must be avoided.

- Difficult passages should never be accepted when an easier passage is possible.

- Distances should be both sensible for conditions and accurately described in publicity.

ISDRA's trail design rules insure that even a musher who has travelled across the country or around the globe to run a race will know what to expect on the trail. The rules also enable the musher and the dogs to train for the conditions they will encounter.

ISDRA race rules are designed to safeguard sled dogs on and off the trail. For example:

248

- Abuse of dogs is strictly prohibited. Anyone who is convicted of animal abuse or neglect shall be barred from racing.
- The Race Marshall must disqualify any team which is unfit or incapable of safety running the race. A veterinarian must be on call for all races. To prevent the spread of disease, the race Veterinarian shall disqualify any team that includes a dog with a contagious disease.
- Use of any substance (from steroids to aspirin) that may affect the performance of a dog is strictly prohibited. ISDRA rules provide for drug testing and disqualification.
- The mushers equipment must comply with race rules. For example, the sled must be equipped with a basket and sled bag capable of safely carrying a dog that is too tired to complete the race.
- The use of choke collars, muzzles and other equipment that might be dangerous to the dogs is prohibited.
- A driver may not leave a dog on the trail for someone else to pick up, nor may a driver replace a dog on the second day of the race with a new dog. This rule is intended to ensure that each dog team is well treated throughout the race.
- While on the race course, the team must stay on the marked trail. Shortcuts are not only cheating, they pose unknown hazards to the teams. The rules also provide rules of the road including "right of way" requirements and passing rules to prevent collisions.

In sum, ISDRA race rules and sanctioning standards are designed and intended to ensure the health and safety of the canine athletes.

International Sled Dog Racing
HC 86 Box 3380, Merrifield, Minnesota 56465 USA
Telephone, Voice Mail, Fax, Fax on Demand Service: (218) 765-4297
E-mail: isdra@uslink.net
Web Site: http://uslink.net/~isdra/

APPENDIX

INSTRUCTIONS FOR CHECKERS

You will be recruited and issued an "Official" vest by the Chief Checker. Transportation to your assigned station will be arranged by the Trail Boss. IMPORTANT: Please be sure to learn from the trail boss or chief checker which trail teams should take at your station, both coming and going, for every class you will be checking. IF YOU DIRECT A TEAM DOWN THE WRONG TRAIL, THE WHOLE CLASS RACE MAY HAVE TO BE DECLARED NULL AND VOID!

PRIMARY DUTY

Stand in the entrance of the trail teams are NOT to take; not too close; not too far. Several checkers, or spectators which you recruit, may stand in a line. A snowmobile may also be used to help block a trail.

At your intersection teams may go out one way and come in another, so be prepared to go back and forth depending on whether teams are coming or going.

When possible, get into position before teams arrive to avoid crossing the trail in front of the team's leaders, which can startle them, costing time.

Point out to the driver which trail the team is to take well ahead of time. STAND QUIETLY AS THE TEAM APPROACHES AND GOES BY.

ASSISTANCE: NON — EMERGENCY

If the leaders want to take the wrong trail, you may move back and forth in front of them to discourage them from going past you. Do not deliberately touch them. If the leaders go past you and need to be pulled onto the correct trail, let the driver do it. If the driver asks you to hold the sled for any reason, run to the sled and hold it with your foot on the brake. If the driver has set the snow hook, DO NOT REMOVE IT unless the driver so directs.

Only the driver touches dogs or lines.

ASSISTANCE: EMERGENCY

An emergency is defined as when a dog or person is hurting or obviously soon will be.

In an emergency, you are encouraged to grab dogs, lines, untangle dogs or do anything else to stop or prevent dogs and drivers from being hurt.

You are particularly encouraged to stop in any way possible and hold a loose team or dog, or a team with the driver dragging. Untangle any hurting dogs; leave minor tangles for the driver to fix.

Any frightened or hurting dog may bite strangers: approach cautiously. If you see a driver in trouble down the trail, go to his/her assistance. A driver will not be penalized for emergency assistance.

ABUSE OF DOGS AND INTERFERENCE

Drivers are allowed to cuss out dogs — but not trail help!

Drivers are not allowed to deliberately strike a dog, no matter how "gently" they hit it.

Drivers are not allowed to interfere with another team.

ANY abuse of dogs or deliberate interference that you see anywhere on the trail should be noted and reported to the Race Marshal and/or the Chief Checker when you come in.

CHECK OFF DRIVERS WHICH PASS YOUR STATION

If you do not recognize the driver, identify him by the number he is wearing. Check off each one as he/she passes. All teams must cover the ENTIRE TRAIL.

When all teams have gone by in the last class, both coming and going, OR when you have been informed that the remaining teams have scratched or turned back, come on in by foot or snowmobile.

PLEASE turn in your "official" vest. THANK YOU FOR YOUR HELP!